PRAISE FOR *LIVING WHILE BLACK*

"In a moment when so many of us are committing to the work of anti-racism, *Living While Black* provides not only a blueprint of tools and strategies for navigating a racist world but guidance for processing the mental and physical effects of everyday anti-Blackness. Speaking to those of us harmed most directly by racism, Kinouani lovingly operationalizes what healing can actually look like and reminds us that not only is joy possible in the face of racial trauma but that it is absolutely necessary for our healing."

—**Yaba Blay,** author of *One Drop:*
Shifting the Lens on Race

"The boldest book on Blackness I have read. The writing is revelatory, necessary, and brilliant. I haven't felt this seen by a text before."

—**Candice Carty-Williams,**
Sunday Times best-selling author of *Queenie*

"An unflinching examination of the daily assaults of anti-Blackness weathering Black bodies, hearts, and minds. With clarity and compassion, Guilaine Kinouani testifies to realities the mental health system has long ignored and denied. This is a must-read for all who profess to be trained in and care about healing."

—**Robin DiAngelo,** *New York Times*
best-selling author of *White Fragility*

"*Living While Black* is an empowering, inspiring, and much-needed work that unapologetically centers Black joy, healing, and resistance. Kinouani unveils how white supremacy harms Black bodies and psyches, and provides a road map to overcoming racial trauma. This book will change and save lives."

—**Crystal M. Fleming,** sociologist and author of *Rise Up!*
How You Can Join the Fight Against White Supremacy

"I believe this powerful and timely book is an essential read for everyone with the very real potential to save Black lives."

—**Temi Mwale,** founder, The 4Front

"When it comes to Guilaine Kinouani, I look forward to nothing short of brilliance. However, I couldn't have been prepared for this stunning piece of work that Guilaine has blessed myself and the world with. I have followed Guilaine for years on social media precisely because of her passionate persistence in breaking open the falsely presented 'impenetrable' nature of how race and mental health interact. This will be a book that I read, recommend, and refer to for years to come. I'm in awe."

—**Kelechi Okafor,** host of *Say Your Mind* podcast

"A vital resource and powerful book—an unmissable read for everyone."

—**Julia Samuel,** *Sunday Times* best-selling author
of *This Too Shall Pass* and *Grief Works*

"An incisive and important book that will change the way you think."

—**Nikesh Shukla,** editor of *The Good Immigrant*
and author of *Brown Baby*

"The book itself is a powerful wake-up call for Black people interested in learning about self-identity and mental well-being. It also offers an important resource for allies to understand and to appreciate what they can do in preventing anti-Blackness in their practice or spheres of influence. It is also a challenge for mainstream therapy professions and psychiatry, what they have been doing to Black people since the creation of the NHS in 1948 in not providing the quality of care and outcomes that Black people need and deserve."

—**Patrick Vernon,** OBE, social commentator and
coauthor of *100 Great Black Britons*

"I've long been a fan of Guilaine's work and was excited for this book. It did not disappoint. Every feeling I've experienced as a Black woman navigating my way through this racist world was articulated here. Texts on race often just expose trauma. The beauty of this was she also offered solutions. This book felt like The Ancestors had enveloped me in a huge hug, whispered in my ear, and gave me the strength to just keep going."

—**Ava Vidal,** comedian

LIVING
WHILE
BLACK

LIVING
WHILE
BLACK

Using Joy, Beauty,
and Connection
to Heal
Racial Trauma

GUILAINE KINOUANI

BEACON PRESS
Boston, Massachusetts

BEACON PRESS
Boston, Massachusetts
www.beacon.org

Beacon Press books
are published under the auspices of
the Unitarian Universalist Association of Congregations.

25 24 23 22   8 7 6 5 4 3 2 1

This book is printed on acid-free paper that meets the uncoated paper
ANSI/NISO specifications for permanence as revised in 1992.

Text design and composition by Kim Arney

Some names and identifying characteristics of the people mentioned
in this work have been changed to protect their identities.

Library of Congress Cataloging-in-Publication Data

Name: Kinouani, Guilaine, 1979– author.
Title: Living while Black : using joy, beauty, and connection to heal
    racial trauma / Guilaine Kinouani.
Description: Boston, Massachusetts : Beacon Press, [2022] | Includes index.
Identifiers: LCCN 2021040483 | ISBN 9780807054581 (hardback) |
    ISBN 9780807054604 (ebook)
Subjects: LCSH: Racism against Blacks. | Racism—Psychological aspects. |
    Blacks—Psychology. | Blacks—Social conditions. | Psychic trauma.
Classification: LCC HT1581 .K56 2022 | DDC 305.896—dc23
LC record available at https://lccn.loc.gov/2021040483

To Misbah, Hayan, Yael, and Malia
To Maman, Papa, and Papa
To the gang of eight
To the ancestors
To us

CONTENTS

CHAPTER 3—BLACK SHAME

CHAPTER 4—BLACK BODIES

CHAPTER 5—RAISING BLACK CHILDREN

CHAPTER 6—WORKING WHILE BLACK

CHAPTER 7—BLACK LOVE

CHAPTER 8—BLACK RESISTANCE

FINAL THOUGHTS—THRIVING WHILE BLACK

INTRODUCTION

Racism causes harm.

Harm to the body. And harm to the mind. Yet it was only in November 2020 that the American Medical Association recognized racism as an urgent threat to public health.[1] Thankfully, many of us did not wait for this penny to drop to tackle its impact. For about fifteen years I have been working therapeutically with people of color, supporting almost exclusively Black people distressed by racism and experiencing racial trauma. *Living While Black* seeks to offer the same support in book form, by presenting some of this work—the politics and personal and professional experiences that underlie my psychology and psychotherapy practice—to help us find connection, hope, and empowerment.

First I want to tell you a little bit about the journey that brought this book to life. I have carved my practice out of the **whiteness** of psychology and psychotherapy.[2] I have carved it out of the thousands of micro and macro experiences of discrimination and Othering I had to navigate. I have refused to ignore this rich set of data, the intellectual gifts contained therein, and their potential to help others heal. Exploring and reflecting on my own lived experience, my lived evidence, has been central to understanding patterns of harm and domination but also patterns of resistance. My scholarship was born out of the documentation of these patterns on Race Reflections, a platform that started as a blog and turned into a social enterprise dedicated to tackling inequality, injustice, and oppression. Women—especially Black women—are socialized to distrust what we know and to be suspicious of our own authority. Often, we stop ourselves from using our gifts, or wait for someone to give us the go-ahead, or to tell us how to start and when to start. I had little support when I decided to set up my practice. What drove me was simply a strong will or perhaps a strong need to have a space where, as a Black woman, a mental health professional, and a psychologist, I could engage with mental health and psychology from the vantage point of being a Black female body in the world, with the richness, complexities, and baggage that this entails.

In distilling these complex learnings, the primary aim of *Living While Black* is to make many of us who often haven't felt this way feel heard, seen, and held. This book seeks to help Black people thrive by first addressing the nuances of Blackness, then creating a tailored self-care plan. The first aspect is achieved via case studies, research, and strategies born out of countless hours of clinical practice and personal reflections, some of it extracted from the work of Race Reflections. The second aspect guides the reader as they self-reflect and prompts them to engage in self-care activities. *Living While Black* is a vital psychology guide for Black people. It is also an anti-racist text for others who simply want to better understand the effects of anti-Black racism so they can do better. And it is a resource for mental health, social care, and medical practitioners working with Black people.

This book sheds a light on the trauma of racism—its impact on both our mental and physical health and its consequences across individuals' lifespans, across generations, and across social contexts. It exposes anti-Black experiences, which society tells us are not occurring or, if they are occurring, are not causing us harm. I want there to be no doubt that racism harms and that racial trauma is real. But, equally, I want to show that it is possible to resist and to practice radical self-care while navigating white supremacy.

The material you will encounter here does not reach most psychology and psychotherapy "teaching" or our collective consciousness. In fact, it is material we have learned to censor. It is therefore rich and heavy material that you are asked to engage with and to honor. Here you will encounter intersectional violence, intergenerational wounds, normalized trauma, everyday resistance, cultural homelessness, structural inequality, and all the intersections of the socioeconomic, the political, the historical, the institutional, the relational, and the psychological. This is the stuff that tends not to reach Black people who seek support for psychological distress. Many mental health professionals still believe politics belongs outside our therapy rooms. That therapy is not political. The whiteness of this position is still to be accepted as a fact, let alone as a problem. Way too many mental health professionals consider social structures and indeed racism to be a distraction from the real issues or a vehicle to the real issues. And for way too many psychotherapists and psychologists, the real issues still lie in our relationship with our mother (imagine a slave in distress at their condition, being asked to reflect on their relationship with their mother, to get to the "real issues").

Over the years, Black people have come to my practice after having been further harmed by those whose job it is to facilitate healing. Psychotherapy and mental health services continue to struggle to work with racism; in fact, they often reproduce it. Mindlessly. The reality is this: If you are Black and those you seek support from are unwilling to look at racism and the trauma it inflicts, these individuals or systems are simply unwilling to look you in the eye. They do not want to see you. They are not prepared to engage with the weight and complexities of our shared and often bloody history. From there, there is usually nowhere to go but an impasse. A wall. The wall of whiteness. It is this absence of thinking that leads to a gap that continues to make racism nearly impossible to address in therapy for way too many.

It is in that gap that some of us are forced to sit while being encouraged to displace Black rage toward our mothers because their capacity to be mothers was affected by the unjust structures within which they mothered us: the abject xenophobia, the racism, the patriarchy, the poverty. I think of my own mom too. Her back is pretty much broken. The social symbolism of a Black woman with a broken back is such a powerful one. So many of the Black women I know have broken backs. Being the mules of society carries such a heavy burden. And so many of their daughters have sore throats or are losing their voices trying to speak words few are prepared to hear. This is what being silenced can do. Black backs have a long history of carrying loads—white loads. And of being flogged for not keeping silent. But we are entitled to take some of the weight off and share it. And we are entitled to speak. And we are entitled to write. In fact, we absolutely must make our voices heard by any means necessary if we are to stand any chance of stopping history from becoming fatality by repetition.

Living While Black is structured in eight chapters, all of which contain an analysis of societal dynamics and offer tools for readers to support themselves and reflect on their own experiences and relationships. Words that appear in boldface are defined in the glossary. The book is organized as follows.

Chapter 1, "Being Black," is an exploration of what being racialized as Black means. From my own lived experience, it offers the context for today's societal dynamics and inequality.

Chapter 2, "Black Minds," looks at how Black people fare in mental health institutions. It examines racial trauma and unpacks the mental health consequences of living within white supremacy.

Chapter 3, "Black Shame," examines shame, a core consequence of racial trauma. It links this shame to racial injustice and to issues of belonging and "homelessness."

Chapter 4, "Black Bodies," links the history of mistreatment of Black people via imperial and colonial violence to everyday acts of Othering. Further, it considers their impact on our bodies.

Chapter 5, "Raising Black Children," focuses on the unique challenges of having a Black child or being a Black parent. It offers prompts for strengthening attachment and mitigating the intergenerational impact of racial trauma.

Chapter 6, "Working While Black," analyzes the dynamics that Black people often face in workplaces. It contextualizes them historically and offers tools for navigating hostile workplace environments.

Chapter 7, "Black Love," explores romance and intimacy and their dynamics in the context of white supremacy. It encourages reflection to help foster more authentic and fulfilling intimate relationships.

Chapter 8, "Black Resistance," offers a roadmap for resistance, drawing on historical examples of rebellion and insurgency. It provides evidence-based tools to help you thrive as you resist white supremacy.

In "Your Radical Self-Care Plan" you will find an action plan with various activities selected to help you connect to your ancestry, your community, and your history and to nurture your body, your mind, and your soul.

Living While Black also provides more specific tools to help you with specific challenges such as managing race-based stress, coping with Black shame, and talking to Black children about race. The title comes from an expression that has been part of racial discourse for decades. The phrase " . . . while Black" is used by Black academics, journalists, writers, and activists in and outside the US to describe the challenges of existing, resisting, and thriving within white supremacy. The term links its origins to a 1999 *Minnesota Law Review* paper by David A. Harris subtitled "Why 'Driving While Black' Matters," which exposed the treatment of Black motorists by the police in 1990s America. The phrase has since been used in a variety of other contexts, such as "birding while Black," "traveling while Black," and "working while Black." It highlights the differing experiences and outcomes of these mundane activities when they are carried out by Black people—because of racism, racial profiling, and the associated risks to our safety, all of which will be explored in this book.

A note on research: The most reliable evidence we have when it comes to Blackness and (mental) health originates from the UK and the US. Inevitably, the research *Living While Black* is based on often comes from these countries. Still, I am a French woman with roots firmly in Africa, so I attempt to keep my outlook on the whole diaspora.

Please also note that the contents of *Living While Black* may sometimes be distressing. You may feel a temptation to disconnect, to put the book down. We know that human beings go to extraordinary lengths to avoid pain, discomfort, and tension. This has resulted in us continuing to refuse to confront the reality of racism. But breaking silences matters. It is always the first step in breaking the cycle of abuse. And we can only break silences if people accept the invitation to hear and see. Here, you are invited. While I primarily address the Black reader directly, and the activities and strategies are focused on our needs, many of the tools will no doubt be helpful to others who experience racism and oppression. I want to again be clear, however, that everyone is invited to come in and reflect on the work we all must do, and to think of what they themselves can do to lighten the load.

Consider this invitation a gift.

CENTERING BLACKNESS

Living While Black unapologetically centers the experience of people racialized as Black. "Racialization" here is about turning certain human beings into "Black" humans. More generally, it is the processes by which a group of people becomes defined by their race. Racialization imposes racial meaning onto previously racially neutral identities in order to reproduce the social order.[3] The belief that humans can be divided into different biological races, characterized by different traits and attributes, came with the commodification of Black people and the expansion of capitalism.[4] Race is a social and historical fabrication or construct linked to colonial and imperial ways of viewing and organizing the world.[5]

We may say that the **social construction** or fabrication of race is the very foundation of racism.[6] But while race is a figment of our imagination, racism is not. Here lies our first contradiction. For our purpose, we'll define racism as a system in which white groups, and those adjacent to them, are placed in a position of power over various other races deemed inferior, and where power is used to maintain privileged access to material resources.[7] The myth of race allows resources to be allocated in ways that privilege white people and thus maintain and legitimize this fantasized racial hierarchy, which, of course, locates Black people as the ultimate Other, at the very bottom. It is that location in the hierarchy that leads to specific patterns of poor and violent treatment commonly referred to as **anti-Blackness.**

The term "Black" remains controversial even among people racialized as Black, even though we are rarely asked what we think about being routinely identified as such. Some of us despise it. The historical load it carries is heavy. Still, we do know that it has been reclaimed at various points in history. Presently, this seems to be the case, as evidenced by the global phenomenon Black Lives Matter, the slogan and movement sparked by anti-Black police brutality. In November 2020, I carried out some research. I wanted to better understand how we relate to the term "Black." In my study, 725 respondents racialized as Black based in the US, the UK, and elsewhere in Europe completed an online survey. A whopping 94 percent said they routinely identified as Black. Despite this, 59 percent still believed that Blackness was an identity imposed on them by society. Opposition to the term was based on its homogenizing nature, its racist associations, and the fact that it erased specific cultural heritage. And 78 percent of the participants agreed that Blackness was a marker of African ancestry.

BLACKNESS AS A BLACK QUEST

Flattening some of the differences that exist within and between different Black groups is a major drawback when theorizing on Blackness. And so, the task of living while Black is a tough one. It is undoubtedly the case that Blackness covers a huge range of ethnic and cultural groups that are heterogenous and have various histories, ethnicities, and **geopolitical** positioning. However, the search for a global connection, for commonalities in experiences, and for a shared fate must be balanced against the risk of diluting important contextual differences.

Some may say that it is an impossible task, and perhaps it is. Still, the politics that inform *Living While Black* and its ethos are diasporic and **Pan-Africanist.** They seek to shed light on challenges we face, because of what we share: the melanin in our skin or even the shape of our bodies, the breadth of our noses, the thickness of our lips, the kinkiness of our hair, which cumulatively or singularly say "Africa" to the world. Say "primitive" to the world. Say "inferior" to the world. Say "dangerous" to the world. Say "disgusting" to the world.

It is primarily this physicality that is used to racialize us, to render our bodies Black, to Blacken them. With white lies. It is this physicality that remains imprisoned by colonial and imperial fantasies and creates some shared experiences among all contextual differences. It is this physicality that carries within it histories of mass atrocities, histories of exploitation, histories of Othering. Histories of silencing. This is what racialization is all about. Of course, the Black body is a body that is or is not gendered. A body that expresses itself through its sexuality and through whom it loves. A body located within a social class system. A body that through birth or geopolitical location can or cannot travel. A body that is or is not disabled. A body that sometimes sits at the intersections of all these systems and many more. Perhaps Blackness is a Black quest. But even if that is all it is, it is worth pursuing.

"Black" versus "black"

There have been ongoing debates concerning the capitalization of "Black" and various arguments for and against that go from the linguistic to the political.[8] In *Living While Black*, I have opted to capitalize it. This is first in recognition that the term refers to people with a shared history and ancestry traceable to Africa, however distant. Secondly and more importantly, and arguably paradoxically, the capitalization seeks to acknowledge that millions of people through the transatlantic slave trade were stripped of national and cultural ties and thus of their ancestral home. This displacement has resulted in the creation of a cultural and psychological home in Blackness that for many is now independent from Africa. This new home, regardless of our individual views and positions, deserves respect and honoring.

CHAPTER 1

BEING BLACK

DISCOVERING ANTI-BLACKNESS

I was four or five when I discovered racism.[1]

I had been playing with my sister and some of the kids from the neighborhood in front of our Parisian *banlieue* tower block, as was customary for poorer families during school holidays or weekends. There were quite a few of us, fifteen or perhaps even more. Children of all backgrounds having fun, skipping, running around, and laughing the summer afternoon away. All of us still quite oblivious to the dire social deprivation we were accustomed to and the hostility created by our existence in France. A white man erupted from a ground floor flat, shouting, clearly aggrieved by the noise we were collectively making. After his rant, he ran directly toward my elder sister and pushed her from behind.

She was six or seven at the most. The white man pushed her so violently that she was propelled forward, fell, and scraped the ground for a few meters. Much of the skin at the back of her arms had gone. Some of the children quickly ran to our second-floor flat to alert my parents. Moments later my mother appeared downstairs to find my sister, other children, and me in tears and my sister covered in blood. Soon she was at the assailant's door, furious and demanding an explanation. She was greeted by a barrage of racist abuse, including the N-word, of course. Rant over, the man proceeded to punch her in the face so forcefully that her skin turned blue-black, one of her eyes became red with blood, and half her face swelled up.

This was not a half-hearted attack. It was a determined, unrestrained, chest-out, full-force, knock-out hit. The kind of punch a charged-up and angry man throws at an enemy assessed to be of considerable force. The kind of heavyweight punch that is full of hatred and carries with it the history of terror. Of white terror. The kind of punch no woman should ever have to bear but that Black women often do. I do not remember much after that. Things have blurred in my memory, but I can still see my mother standing after the assault. Standing tall, defiant, and in dignified silence. Not a single tear. Not a word in retort. Although I do not remember this, I am told that the white man was arrested minutes later, knife in hand, threatening to kill her in front of an audience of distraught children. Imagine the scene. The loudness, the chaos, the screams, the powerlessness.

SCHOOLING WHILE BLACK

Later, I was exposed to a different kind of racism when my mother got into a dispute with my primary school.[2] Since I was born in February, and as a result missed the official cutoff point for admission by a few days or so, the decision as to whether I could start or not was at the discretion of the school. While, for white children, starting school a little early was rarely an issue, the school took umbrage that my mother thought her child was ready to start. My entry was barred—a rare occurrence. My mother challenged the school, mainly out of principle, as she knew that she and I were being treated differently. The school officials dug in their heels and decided that the only way to prove I was sufficiently intelligent—or "cognitively ready"—was to test my IQ, seeming almost certain that I would not overcome this hurdle. I was subjected to a battery of tests by a team of psychologists. Then they wrote their report. The school's appointed psychologists had found that I had a much higher "intelligence" than average and was, in fact, advanced for my age. Reluctantly, they allowed me in.

Fast-forward to my teens. During a philosophy class, I questioned Descartes's concept of **dualism**. The teacher responded by calling me a monkey who was incapable of thinking and was, instead, looking at the finger of Descartes, as Descartes was pointing to the sun. Then, in high school, I had a history and geography teacher who taught us all about the important job France did in civilizing and enlightening Africa from the Dark Ages, as part of a module on **colonialism**. The course was so whitewashed, uncritical, and steeped in white nostalgia that it was psychologically violent. In the end, students of color were excused, off the record, from attending this class. A compromise to avoid the disturbance of our questions and critical eyes or to have to rethink the curriculum.

Throughout my teens I watched my mother continue to battle white teachers' low and stereotypical expectations. None of us had "what it took" to go to university. Against all "odds" and our "limited" intellectual capabilities, we now count among ourselves as siblings: one physicist, two economists, one accountant, and—wow—a psychologist. That would be me. Seven out of eight of us did go to university, and most of us obtained postgraduate qualifications. For my part, I studied English at La Sorbonne in Paris straight after my baccalaureate. As part of an American civilization class, we were taught that the US was the number one economic power in the world due to its high national IQ but that as a nation it was still being held back because of the low IQ of African Americans.

WHITE WOMEN AND LIBERAL RACISM

Afterwards, I found myself studying psychology in Britain. There I encountered a different kind of racism. One I was ill-equipped to deal with or understand. The liberal kind. Insidious, normalized, and shifty. The kind of racism middle-class white women excel at.[3] The kind of racism that hides even from the mind and body that harbors it. It hides behind decorum, impeccable manners, and professionalism. Professional racism, we may say. The kind of racism that knows better than you and constantly rationalizes itself away, weaponizing innocence and good intentions.

I learned what white women as a group can and do get away with in white institutions. Whenever I reflect on these times, it is the faces of white middle-class women I see. Smiling. I learned that society will not recognize racist violence if it is not obvious. If it is not a white man pushing you from behind or punching you in the face. I learned that hurting the egos of middle-class professional white women, by asking them to reflect on their racism, is one of the most treacherous things a Black woman can do. I learned that equality and diversity policies are primarily used to hide racism and often to protect institutions from their racism. My years in academic psychology have, beyond a shadow of a doubt, been the most distressing years of my adult life. I somehow survived; in fact, I did much more than survive: I thrived. I too still stand, dignified. But not silent. There are various ways to resist.

ON WRITING MYSELF IN

I thought long and hard about whether I should write myself into this book. I am a therapist, but therapy is political. The violent structures within which I exist and do therapy, and the experiences you will be introduced to later in the book, are not separate from my life or yours—whether you know it or not. Or like it or not. We are part of the world we write about; the world we write about lives inside us.

Too often Black people are told directly or indirectly that we must keep quiet when we experience racial injustices—that is, if these experiences are even recognized as racial injustices.[4] We are told that if we are upset about racist experiences—that is, if they are accepted as racist experiences—there is never anything to be distressed about. If we ever get distressed, we are reminded that we must be more resilient. More robust. More moved on. More mature. Speak not, we are told, but if you must speak, speak gently. Cry not, but if you must cry, cry silently. Write not, but if you must write, write impersonally. Exist not, but if you must exist, be as invisible as you can be. Take up as little space as you can take. Let us not see you, let us not hear you, and let us forget you exist, because your existence reminds us of who we are.

THE ROOTS OF OUR RESISTANCE

We owe so much of our spirit of survival and resistance to our fore-mothers, famous and anonymous alike. Those who have struggled in the cotton or sugarcane fields of "new worlds" and those who have fought for independence from colonialism. But also all the others who have bowed their heads, scrubbed, and sacrificed their dignity and at times their health to give us the best chances in life. Those who have carried white bodies on their back as carers and caregivers while being spat at so that we could get a chance at having an education. Often the same who just decades later were shipped back like unwanted cargo— those caught up in the Windrush debacle and the so-called hostile environment in Britain, as though they had ever known any other kind of environment there. Their dignity and resilience, their beauty, we must never forget. The gifts they have left us will forever be with us.

So, what I know is the sum of where I have walked, where I stand in the world, and what I have learned as a therapist. However, the multigenerational histories that birthed me have birthed this book too. French people sometimes call people like me, these reported "second generation of migrants," *les déracinés*, or "those who are uprooted." Trees pulled out from their roots. Trees, it is therefore assumed, without a firm foundation, with no grounding. But our roots are more solid than they appear. They simply extend beyond the boundaries of one nation. They branched out from and into various countries and cultures. But the farther away from the soil a tree extends, the thicker and stronger the roots need to be for its branches to survive and flourish. It is France that has sought to uproot us from our Frenchness.

In the same way, so many Black people in the UK and throughout the world are reminded of their Otherness by being constantly asked "Where are you really from?" in white spaces. The assumption, of course, is that they do not belong or, at least, that they do not belong "here." Their home is elsewhere. No one subjected to chronic experiences of racism in their homeland can ever fully feel at home in their home, particularly when these Othering experiences occur in their tender years and are repeated throughout their entire life. But it is where the story starts.

"I CAN'T BREATHE!"

Have you ever tried to swallow your cries? This is what imposed silences feel like. Racism makes breathing laborious. It makes it hard to breathe. On May 25, 2020, George Floyd, a Black American man, was arrested on suspicion of attempting to buy a pack of cigarettes with a counterfeit twenty-dollar bill. He was publicly suffocated to death by Derek Chauvin, a white police officer. The arrest was filmed by a witness, showing Chauvin kneeling on Floyd's neck for over eight minutes while handcuffed and face down on the ground. Seeing death approaching, Floyd repeatedly pleaded for his life: "I can't breathe." "They will kill me."[5] The world watched in horror as his prediction came true. He was killed on the street and in plain sight. Some might say, like a dog. The death of Floyd hit the world hard. It turned into a catalyst for global protests, demonstrations against anti-Black police brutality, and demands for racial justice and the abolition of the police.[6] However, the murder of George Floyd did more than trigger unrest and street disturbances. It brought to light the collective distress and despair among Black people in the US and well beyond.[7]

The trauma of racism was laid bare for us all to see. Anger and sadness combined forces. Calls for changes in policing, accountability, and complete social reformation swept many Western nations. All with their own histories of anti-Black police murders. Along with the name of George Floyd, the names of others resonated in the streets: Justice for Trayvon Martin. Justice for Eric Garner. Justice for Sandra Bland. Justice for Breonna Taylor! The name of Adama Traoré was screamed on the streets of France together with other names that started to be called in my childhood, such as the name Makomé M'Bowolé. In the UK, Olaseni Lewis, Sheku Bayoh, Kingsley Burrell, Rashan Charles, Sean Rigg, Roger Sylvester, Joy Gardner, Cynthia Jarrett, and so many more who were suffocated to death or died after contact with the police or other government services. So many names. Too many to attempt to recall here.

Tears, screams, and direct action took over so many nations. "Black Lives Matter" appeared on placards. Message after message of angst reached my mailbox: "I can't stop crying"; "I have not slept in days"; "How do I prepare my children for this?"; "I am exhausted"; "I do not know how to talk to my white friends about Living While Black." Each email hit me right in the heart. Holding on to hope can sometimes feel impossible. It is so easy to feel as though one is one step away from falling into the depths of madness or despair while being expected to keep it all under wraps. Writing, and especially writing myself in, is my act of protest. **Anti-Blackness** is not an academic project. We live our theories, but our lives are not theoretical. We are all involved here, so we must connect. We must connect the dots. And again, we must simply connect.

Over the years, I have learned too that each time I dig deep into my own experience, unpack it, explore it, bear witness to it by putting it into words, somebody—often several people—miles and miles away, thanks me for writing about *them*. For making their story known. The more intricate the details, the more of myself I give, the more strangers, complete strangers, say they see themselves in my words. But writing and reading is simply not enough. It is not enough to keep ourselves at the head or cerebral level.

CONNECTING AS AN ACT OF LOVE

There is something powerfully humanizing in those connections that writing with honesty brings, that writing and reading with an open heart creates. I think ultimately connecting with our experiences allows us to connect with the experience of others and for others to connect with theirs and so forth. Understanding the lived experience of one single individual gets us much closer than anything else to grasping the global phenomenon and machinery that is racism. Therefore, stories of survival, of defiance, of resistance allow us all to better understand hate but also to better understand love. Out of this connection is born a recognition of our shared humanity, a powerful antidote to oppression, if one does accept the invitation.

We have worked hard in our society to make love irrelevant and obsolete in mainstream social justice work and politics. And to make social justice and politics irrelevant to psychology and mental health. There is often an implicit contempt for matters of the heart. We have become suspicious of human feelings, arguably for good reasons. However, without transparently sharing the struggles and the triumphs of our lives, there cannot be understanding. Without transparency, there cannot be a connection. Connection between the reader's world and the words of the author.

Interconnectedness is therefore a shared fate. I believe that every text is in some way autobiographical, whether openly or not. Who we are, even if only in traces, is always in there, present in between the words.

My position, as I hope will become clearer in the rest of the book, is that connection matters. And while connection matters, love matters even more. And, conversely, without connection, there can be no love. Love for the self but also love for the Other. Touching hearts is no guaranteed way to radical social transformation, but it is part of the revolution. It is no coincidence that white groups go to extraordinary lengths to avoid being touched. And one way to avoid being touched is to be oblivious to the realities and lived experiences of racism. To erase them from the collective mind. To normalize willful amnesia. To constantly reconfigure one's memory to set it free of the violence and suffering that is all around us. Suffering that would again otherwise force that human connection. Connection, therefore, makes detachment, dissociation, and complicity much more difficult. It is harder to shoot someone in the face—literally and figuratively—while staring into their eyes.

So, this transparency is, first, intended to help you contextualize the issues raised in this book and to grasp why it has been written. It is to help Black readers know they are not alone. Then, it is to connect our lived experience to **anti-racism**, or the act of actively seeking to dismantle or combat racism—and to love. A deep love for Black people and anybody else who is oppressed around the world underscores this project. But also, perhaps, an unconscious desire to provoke love in those who do us harm, perhaps despite themselves. This love aspiration is not naïve, romantic, or immature. Nor is it the kind of love that often requires that Black people and those harmed by racism should forever turn the other cheek. No, it is the kind of love that is political. A Black feminist kind of love. The love I am talking about is a militant one. One that cannot be separated from justice or a desire to repair and rebuild a fairer world. A love that requires showing up and being there. A love that is all about daring to see the Other in their full humanity. A love that invokes compassion. Without compassion, we cannot hope to be motivated enough to change. We cannot hope to hope.

The author bell hooks defines this love as "a combination of care, knowledge, responsibility, respect, trust, and commitment."[8] Perhaps it *is* possible to force change. No revolution was ever built on love alone, no matter how radical. Still, sustaining change requires more than coercion. Coercion breeds resistance and rebellion, and no one on this planet knows this better than Black people. We cannot force connection. We cannot legislate love. Therefore, bell hooks teaches us that power breeds lovelessness. Anti-Blackness, we may say, is a defense against love. It is a way to avoid the intimacy and connection to the self and to others. A sophisticated and atrociously costly way to avoid seeing and being seen. I hope sharing a bit of my experience will allow you to connect to the human that I am. To humanity. And, by extension, to see the humanity of those whose bodies look like mine. Anti-Blackness is a matter of life and death. I hope that connection will help dismantle all the walls so many put around themselves to avoid being touched by us and help them choose life over death. I hope because we need to hope—without hope, there can be no resistance.

SUMMARY

1.

Experiences of racism for Black people are ubiquitous. They happen across contexts and often throughout our lifespan. They shape our life trajectories and worldview, including what we come to believe about the world and what we're able to see in the world, as well as our vocational and/or professional interests or talents.

2.

As a result, transparency and reflexivity are important qualities for anyone who wants to understand race. Writing with honesty and integrity challenges whiteness. It also aims to help the reader better understand the personal context of *Living While Black* and the lived experiences that can lead to racial trauma.

3.

Connection is fundamental to love and to authentic human relationships, yet racism forces disconnection at various levels, most fundamentally between Black people and people who perform anti-Blackness. Anti-racism must therefore involve building authentic connections.

4.

It is not possible to separate the writer from where they stand in the world, in the same way that it is not possible to separate the mind from the body. As we will see in the chapters to come, reconnecting mind, body, and soul is central to healing wounds from racial trauma.

....

The next chapter, "Black Minds," considers the institutional context and inequalities in relation to Black mental health and looks at the ways we can understand racial trauma.

RACE REFLECTIONS

You have learned about the personal context of *Living While Black*, including my experience of racial injustice and how it influences my worldview and work on racism. This section gives you the opportunity to reflect on your own personal context and develop reflective skills. These are needed not only to engage with the current chapter but also to prepare you for the rest of the book.

Gearing yourself toward self-care

Engaging with racism and injustice is a risk factor for psychological distress. For this reason, it is vital that, as you go through the book, you actively seek to take care of your body, your mind, and your soul by engaging in self-care. I define it as the deliberate steps we take to practice self-protection, self-nurture, self-soothing, and self-kindness. Please reflect on what the definition evokes in you and the kinds of activities you could engage in to fulfill all elements of the definition. Then ask yourself this question: what do you need to maintain a sense of hope?

_____

_____

_____

_____

_____

**What have you learned from this chapter
that you have found most challenging?**

You may want to explore the images, thoughts, and physical responses that came to you and explore what they might take you back to. Please use the Race Reflections reflective model (p. 183) to help you.

_____

_____

_____

_____

_____

When was your first encounter with racism?

What were the circumstances and how old were you? Try to remind yourself of as much detail as possible. Connect to the feelings you experienced at the time. Name them. As you connect, it is helpful to become attuned to how your body responds to these racialized memories. Many will be embodied; treat these feelings as data and be curious about them. What can they teach you about racial injustice? Could they help you recognize racism? What do they tell you about self-care?

_____

_____

_____

_____

_____

Reflect on your identity development

Racial identity development *concerns our growing sense of belonging or identification with a racial group, here Blackness. It typically occurs in early adolescence and when we go from a place of racial obliviousness to, we could say, racial consciousness. The box overleaf summarizes the model of William E. Cross Jr., an American scholar and researcher on racial identity. Please review the stages and consider what stage you may be at and what events and actions you may use to support your position.*

_____

_____

_____

_____

_____

Racial Identity Development

Cross's 5 Stages of Black Racial Identity Development

- Stage 1—Pre-encounter: "it is better to be white."

- Stage 2—Encounter: forced acknowledgement of racism.

- Stage 3—Immersion/Emersion: active avoidance of "symbols" of whiteness.

- Stage 4—Internalization: connected to Black peers; willing to engage with Whites.

- Stage 5—Internalization-Commitment: personal sense of what it means to be Black; commitment to the welfare of Blacks as a whole; comfort interacting with Whites; positive racial identity.

Credit: William E. Cross Jr., *Shades of Black: Diversity in African American Identity* (Philadelphia: Temple University Press, 1991).

ACTION POINT

GET A REFLECTIVE JOURNAL

You are encouraged to keep a reflective journal throughout your engagement with *Living While Black* and ideally
after. Your reflective journal is where you will record your
thoughts and reactions. If you do not feel that writing is
the best way to engage in your learning, feel free to use an
alternative way to record your thoughts, feelings, and reflections (including embodied responses). Your first action
is simply to secure such a journal.

CHAPTER 2

BLACK MINDS

As human beings we are designed to feel safe and to feel like we belong. Therefore, we can never really get used to or become fully desensitized to racism, however hard we may try. We often simply end up succeeding at denying, burying, or dissociating from the pain it causes. In this chapter we consider the institutional context of **Black mental health**. We look at well-documented inequalities, but we also go much further. We consider the "Black experience" when it comes to **mental health** systems. An experience that sits at the intersection of various systems of oppression.

BLACK MINDS, WHITE INSTITUTIONS

Case study: Mike

*Mike is a young Black man who has spent his life in London after coming to England to seek asylum due to war in his country of origin. Growing up, Mike hated school. Whenever trouble occurred, teachers usually assumed he was responsible. Mike felt treated as though he was not expected to do well, unlike other children. He eventually believed he was not as clever as the other students and began to feel out of place in school. In his early teens, Mike started avoiding school and skipping school, which resulted in him getting expelled. His white peers were given warnings for similar infractions. To fill his days, Mike spent much time on the streets of London. At about seventeen, he experimented with cannabis. Shortly after, he started "hearing voices" and was first diagnosed with "**drug-induced*** *psychosis," then with **schizophrenia**, and was compulsorily detained under the **Mental Health Act (1983)**. Mike noticed many other Black men in the hospital and resented being there. Many of these other Black men had been detained in mental health services following the involvement of the police. Very few Black men were in therapy or were given the chance to talk about their lived experience. When racism was broached, staff often changed the subject or became defensive. Mike had to endure racial slurs on the ward, mainly from other mental health service users. Mike remained in the hospital for about a month. Weeks after his discharge, he got into a confrontation with the police. He claimed to have been stopped by the police three times in the same day. He also reported having been stopped the day before. Mike had recurrently seen police officers target other Black kids for searches. He became defiant and angry and refused to comply. The situation escalated, and Mike ended up being physically restrained by three officers. He was arrested and eventually charged with common assault. In court, no one seemed interested in his experience with the police or with schools. Instead, he was deemed to have a problem with authority and sentenced to six months in prison, where he became unwell again. From there, he was transferred to a **medium secure unit**, which is a mental health service providing treatment for those who have been arrested or committed a crime, diagnosed with psychiatric disorders, and/or deemed to pose high risks of harm to themselves or others. He was compulsorily detained for several years in the unit. It was there that I met him, and we started doing some therapeutic work.*

Over the years, I have worked with several young men with stories similar to Mike's. The bulk of this work focused on helping these young men unpack their experience of racism, rebuild trust (including toward themselves), and process their anger. This story speaks to the multitude of inequalities and violence Black people often experience when dealing with mental health services. It also reveals the layers of trauma that can coexist in one individual. Here, the trauma of war, abuse, and **structural racism** all lead to an extraordinarily complex picture when it comes to Black mental health.

In our quest to understand the challenges Black people experience with our mental health services and the apparent excess of "**mental health problems**" in our communities, we must remember that challenges exist in relation to these conceptualizations. The Eurocentricity and failure to consider the historical and sociopolitical realities of Blackness has been the cause of criticism for decades. Wherever possible I prefer to use the terms "distress," "psychological distress," or "suffering" when considering the "Black experience." This is to avoid being limited to a medical framework of understanding our experiences or to individualistic lenses. However, when drawing on findings from the existing literature, medical terminology cannot be avoided entirely since the **medical model** is still the dominant one for understanding psychological suffering in the West.

Our definitions of mental health will vary from person to person. However, generally when we talk about mental health we are talking about our subjective sense of well-being, and when we talk about "mental health problems," we are referring to difficulties in relating to ourselves, others, and/or to the world. Or we refer to feelings, thoughts, and behaviors that have adverse effects on our ability to lead fulfilling lives. (Again, these definitions are not without problems, and we will return to them later in the chapter.)

When it comes to mental health, stark inequalities exist across racial lines. To assess them, the UK Department of Health (DoH) has historically considered three main classes of inequality across racial groups:

1. Inequality in terms of access or in the route different racial groups take to access support.
2. Inequality in terms of experience or how various groups experience mental health services.
3. Inequality in terms of outcomes that are centered on what happens to us clinically once we get into services, such as whether we "recover" and go on to live fulfilling lives or whether we end up being "revolving door patients."[1]

The inequitable treatment of Black people has been documented at all three levels. The list of mental health inequality is long and seriously disturbing.

To summarize, Black groups are subject to more adverse and coercive mental health practices than any other ethnic group in the UK. We are more likely to

- get mental health care and treatment by force, such as through the involvement of the police[2]
- be detained within psychiatric hospitals against our will[3]
- be assessed or stereotyped as dangerous more than any other group in the UK and less likely to be offered psychotherapy
- spend years in and out of mental health institutions and be overmedicated[4]
- be diagnosed with having **severe and enduring mental health problems** such as psychosis more often than white and Asian groups[5]
- not receive support for a "common mental health problem" (e.g., anxiety and depression) yet just as likely to experience them

We still experience racism in mental health services and are often reluctant to engage with them, which leads to cycles of coercion, fear, and stigma.

The picture does not appear much more favorable in the US, where it has been acknowledged that Black people are much less likely than white groups to be the recipients of mental health support despite their needs.[6]

In the US

- Black groups are less likely than other racial groups to seek mental health support.[7]
- Although Black Americans may overall be less likely to experience "depression," when depressed it is more likely that their condition will be chronic and that they will suffer higher levels of disability than whites.[8]

- Black Americans with severe depression are more likely to be misdiagnosed as having schizophrenia, likely due to racial bias and racism.[9]
- Like in the UK, one of the most consistent racial inequalities is the disproportionately high rate of psychotic diagnoses among Black Americans despite the lack of evidence for biological predisposition.[10]
- Alarmingly, the suicide rate of Black children is rising, which is the case for no other racial group.[11]

These inequities are concerning enough as they are, but they do not end here. We, as a group, are also more likely to die in mental health institutions. This context laid the foundation for the death of David "Rocky" Bennett.

Case study: Rocky

*In 1998, mental health patient David "Rocky" Bennett, a Black Rastafarian man, was killed while physically restrained on a psychiatric ward. This death had a seismic cultural impact for those in the UK mental health system. The independent inquiry found that David had died as a direct result of prolonged face-down physical restraint and because of the amount of force used by five members of staff. David had been restrained face-down on the floor for twenty-five minutes. Restrained in what is called a "**prone position**." A position only to be used for the shortest of instances to minimize the risk of injury or death. Three minutes was eventually recommended by the inquiry.[12]*

The inquiry into David's death found a catalogue of failings, including the stereotyping of David. It also showed that there was no real attempt to engage with his family as part of the treatment of his "psychosis" diagnosis during a period of almost twenty years. David was repeatedly treated as "a nuisance to be contained" by over-medication. His cultural, social, and religious needs were not considered when viewing his reactions and experiences on the ward. David had suffered from racist abuse throughout his stay in the hospital. But as staff were unaware of the impact of cumulative racist abuse, David was not offered support. In fact, his complaints were often not even recorded. David's race-based distress was ignored until his death.

Over the years, I have pictured David "Rocky" Bennett's last moments in my head. The findings of the inquiry were published around the time I was starting as a mental health professional. I have repeatedly imagined what the scene may have been like as he lay on the floor, his life slipping away. I imagined him thrashing about, trying to break free. I imagined him gasping for air and repeatedly pleading for his life. David was killed in a way that painfully and eerily presaged the death of George Floyd in the United States. I can easily imagine David saying, "I can't breathe," however muffled his voice might have been. There is evidence that, like George Floyd, David was heard saying "They are trying to kill me."

David Bennett's death has parallels with another Black death.[13] Today, few in the UK are unfamiliar with the death of Stephen Lawrence, the Black teenager stabbed to death in 1993 in an unprovoked racist attack.[14] I was not living in Britain when Stephen was murdered, but his murder is one of the first things I learned about this country when I migrated here. The poor handling of the police investigation into his murder led to delayed and only partial justice for the boy and his loved ones. The report on the public inquiry led by Sir William Macpherson was published in 1999 and found the police force to be institutionally racist.

This sent shock waves into the country, challenging its long-held self-image as a tolerant and racially blind liberal haven. Although the findings from the inquiry led to significant cultural changes in attitudes toward law enforcement and in community policing, the Lawrences only obtained a semblance of justice. Only two of Stephen's murderers were eventually imprisoned following a change in the British **double jeopardy law**. It was after almost two decades of tireless campaigning by his parents and an unsuccessful private prosecution that in 2012 David Norris and Gary Dobson were finally convicted of murder and received life sentences. The murder of Stephen Lawrence and the subsequent botched investigation left an indelible blood stain on the nation's consciousness.

One factor that unites the deaths of David Bennett and Stephen Lawrence is government services' refusal to consider the centrality of racism in the tragedy that unfolded and in the deaths of these two young Black men. The refusal, overt or covert, to confront the lived reality of racism in the lives of Black people is a tell-tale sign of institutional racism. The refusal to take seriously the testimonies of those directly impacted by racism kills. Our society is still in denial about the impact of racism. And the refusal to see racism often translates into the refusal to see us as human beings. David and Stephen were not seen in their full humanity. They never stood a chance.

Contact between the police and Black groups has become a public health concern. It has the real potential to damage the health of individuals "stopped and searched." Over the years I have encountered hundreds of young Black men in community, forensic, and clinical settings. I can say, with no hesitation, that young Black men's experience of the police has been one of the most virulent and recurrent issues I have been presented with. Expectedly, it was often accompanied by feelings of rage, despair, helplessness, distrust, and alienation. Feelings strongly associated with psychological distress.

We now have some research findings to support this clinical experience. We have limited data in the UK; however, in the US, greater anxiety and even trauma symptoms have been found among those "stopped and frisked." This distress is closely related to how intrusive contact with the police is, the number of "stop and frisk" events reported over one's lifetime, and the sense of injustice. We also have some research that evidences that witnessing the police killing of unarmed Black Americans has predictable detrimental effects on the collective mental health of Black American adults in the general population. Researchers have called these the "spillover" effects of police brutality.[15]

Mental health inequalities have not abated. In fact, they are getting worse. There is a high proportion of Black people who have come to find death in places where they should have found solace and safety, killed by those meant to care for them. Further US data shows that people with mental health problems may be up to sixteen times more likely to be killed by the police.[16] The intersection of Blackness and disability and that of Blackness and psychological distress are two of the deadliest. Imagine living in a world where psychological suffering puts you at risk of further suffering and increases the chance of you experiencing violent racism, if not death? It is a hard thought to hold.

PSYCHOTHERAPY AND RACISM

I have studied psychology for about seven years. In these years, I have never received a single lecture on racism, let alone on racial trauma. This is despite the inquiry into the death of David Bennett recommending that a better understanding of the impact of racism is central to reducing racial inequalities in the mental health system and the ongoing inequalities we have just covered.

I wrote in chapter 1 about the risks that still exist in calling out racism and the dynamics this can set in motion; these exist in the mental health field too. White ignorance plays a massive part. And so, troublingly, in my clinical and research work I have come across the very same silencing experiences among Black patients who attempted to bring racism into their psychotherapy. Unsurprisingly, Black people's voices and lived experiences are virtually absent from the psychology and psychotherapy literature and research. The difficulty of psychology and mental health professionals in addressing and working with racism is well-documented.[17]

Through this absence, psychology and, more broadly, mental health services may at best be charged with complicity in the active reproduction of this conspiracy of silence, and at worst with facilitating psychological harm and re-traumatization.[18] The lack of understanding of the centrality of racism in Black people's experience of psychological distress has dire consequences. Not the least of these is the normalizing of abuses of power in society, thus the upholding of white supremacy. This lack of understanding also contributes to distrust, stigma, and fear of mental health services. It feeds racial inequalities in the mental health system. Not treating racial trauma and racism seriously renders psychology and psychotherapy vulnerable to accusations of institutional racism. And institutional racism is not just about "cultural incompetence"—it is also about a continued tolerance of dehumanizing practices and a systemic failure to challenge and change racially discriminatory patterns of care.[19]

DEFINING RACIAL TRAUMA

While society refuses to see racism, racism continues to harm us. There is little doubt that the lived experience of racial discrimination is a significant factor in the over-prevalence of psychological distress that can be found within Black groups. It has been linked to various manifestations of psychological suffering, including depression, psychosis, anxiety, and trauma.[20]

But what is racial trauma? The American Psychological Association (APA) refers to trauma as an "emotional response to a terrible event like an accident, rape or natural disaster." The APA adds that long-term reactions include unpredictable emotions, flashbacks, strained relationships, and even physical symptoms like headaches or nausea. Immediately after the event, shock and denial are typical.

To understand the case for racial trauma, we also need to understand **post-traumatic stress disorder (PTSD)**. It is the major trauma diagnosis and is a condition characterized by the reexperiencing of a traumatic event (or events), hypervigilance, or what we may refer to as being hyperalert to possible dangers and threats, and the avoidance of reminders of the trauma.

According to the latest version of the *Diagnostic and Statistical Manual of Mental Disorders*, criterion A for a diagnosis of PTSD entails a traumatic event or stressor that must involve exposure to death, injury, or sexual violence, or the threat thereof, in one of the following ways:

1. direct exposure
2. indirect exposure (e.g., witnessing a stressor and/or traumatic event occurring to someone else)

3. hearing about violent/accidental event(s) someone close
   experienced
4. being repeatedly exposed to graphic details of a stressor/trau-
   matic event[21]

Having met the requirements of criterion A, an individual is assessed
using additional criteria, essentially as follows:

- **Criterion B:** recurrently reliving the stressor/traumatic event
- **Criterion C:** avoiding reminders of the stressor/traumatic event
- **Criterion D:** a negative change in thoughts/feelings after the
  stressor/traumatic event
- **Criterion E:** trauma-related arousal and reactivity
- **Criterion F:** symptoms present for at least one month
- **Criterion G:** evidence of distress or impairment in functioning
  (e.g., difficulties at work or school or both)
- **Criterion H:** symptoms caused by trauma, not by medication,
  substance use, or other illness

Thus, broadly speaking, trauma describes responses to frightening
events. It refers to a long-lasting, overwhelming feeling of being unsafe
and a sense of distress that follows exposure. Although we have known
for decades that racism can cause traumatic responses, it is only recently
that the links between racial discrimination, racism, and trauma have
received mainstream clinical attention. Part of the case for racial trauma
as a conceptual tool is that so many people distressed by racism were
not meeting the diagnostic criteria for PTSD, which currently hinges
on the threat to one's life. Many clinicians have argued and found em-
pirically (via scientific research) that trauma symptoms can exist in the
absence of threat to life. Smaller and less extreme but repeated experiences of discrimination and Othering can cumulate into significant
psychological difficulties, "psychiatric" presentations, and experiences
that often mirror PTSD (and other "psychiatric disorder") "symptoms."
    Racial trauma is therefore a framework to describe the physical and
emotional responses that can follow exposure to racism and that may,

clinically speaking, include any of the "symptoms" listed above and indeed many more. The core defining feature of racial trauma frameworks is racism and its various manifestations as the cause of psychological distress.

RACE-BASED TRAUMATIC STRESS INJURY

"Race-based traumatic stress injury" is a framework created by Robert Carter, a Black American psychologist.[22] The framework defines trauma as the emotional pain that a person may feel after encounters with racism. According to this framework, the way people experience encounters with racism can vary from one individual to another. Responses depend on an individual's background or health and how they make sense of what has happened to them.

A person who interprets their racial encounter as extremely negative, sudden, or uncontrollable may start to show signs of stress and trauma. Carter suggests that for trauma to be present, the reaction or symptoms need to include psychological intrusion (e.g., flashbacks), avoidance of reminders of the initial distressing event, and "arousal" (e.g., being easily startled). According to Carter, the signs of racial trauma may be exhibited emotionally, physiologically, cognitively, behaviorally, or in combination of two or more of these. One may express the trauma through anxiety, anger, rage, depression, low self-esteem, shame, and guilt. Although not a "formal" diagnosis in dominant psychiatric categorization systems, race-based traumatic stress injury has gained much traction as a clinical framework, particularly in the US.

A further conceptualization of racial trauma is that of African American psychologist Shelly Harrell.[23] She offers a six-level framework that examines the ways in which we are harmed by racism:

1. **Racism-related life events.** These are racial assaults and acts of racial discrimination that target us directly and unequivocally.
   For example: when we are called a racist term or assaulted because we are Black.

2. **Vicarious racism (indirect exposure to racism).**
   For example: when we hear stories of racism occurring to those around us or witness it.

3. **Daily racist micro-stressors.** These are subtle, normalized, and ambiguous acts of racist denigration, the kinds of acts and words that many would refer to as microaggressions today. *For example:* being followed in a store or being repeatedly asked "Where are you from?"

4. **Chronic contextual stress.** This is the mere awareness of structural race inequality and unequal distribution of resources.
   For example: being exposed to racial inequality statistics via the media or popular culture.

5. **Collective experiences of racism: Witnessing the racism inflicted on one's racial group.**
   For example: witnessing the murder of Black people at the hands of the state.

6. **Transgenerational transmission of group trauma: Aspects of oppression related to historical events are passed on.**
   For example: when our parents share tips about surviving white supremacy.

The last three levels of Dr. Harrell's framework deal with the impact of racism at group level, something that tends to evade most conversations on racism and racial trauma. They help us to understand the Black Lives Matter movement and why so many Black people around the world were so distraught by the murder of George Floyd. This framework is helpful since it highlights two important things: First, the chronic nature of racial trauma, which sets it apart from most other forms of trauma. Second, it stresses the collective harm that racism can inflict. Other frameworks exist for this purpose, and we will cover these later in the book.

RACIAL TRAUMA: SIGNS AND MANIFESTATIONS

How we define racial trauma and the framework we use will invariably shape what we pay attention to when it comes to signs and manifestations, and indeed what we consider to be signs and manifestations of racial trauma. We have now examined various forms of racism, and throughout the book you will be encouraged to think well beyond the individual when conceptualizing racial trauma (while still holding the individual's experience in mind). Thinking about signs and manifestations is no different. The table below presents some of the signs and manifestations of racism I have formulated:

Signs and manifestations of racial trauma

Individual level	Family level	Community level
• Distrust of white people • Shame of heritage and internalized racism • Hypervigilance and cultural paranoia • Substance misuse • Anxiety • Low mood/ depression • Low self-esteem • Excessive work and perfectionism • Self-harming behaviors • Fear of speaking out; self-silencing	• Distrust of white people • Raising children to comply and work "twice as hard" • Attachment and/ or relationship difficulties • Harsh punishment/ discipline of children • Child neglect and abuse • Repetition of cycles of neglect/abuse intergenerationally • Silence and difficulty naming racism • Fear a loved one may come to harm/ overprotection	• Acceptance of the status quo • Learned helplessness • Identification with the aggressor • Intra-group conflicts (through displacement of aggression) • Scapegoating "transgressors" (e.g., those who don't toe the white line or keep silent) • Enactment of other axes of oppression (e.g., ableism and homophobia) • Reproduction of historical relational scripts such as subservience • Respectability and assimilative politics

The above is not an exhaustive list. Instead, it aims to get you thinking about the multitude of ways in which racial trauma can manifest itself and be recognized. The signs will vary depending on the individual and the social context, in the same way that the impact of the same psychological stressor might look quite different in different people. How we process racist incidents, our history, past adverse events, family survival, and survival strategies—all these factors and more intersect to create responses to racism and therefore racial trauma presentations.

INTERGENERATIONAL WOUNDS: THE BAGGAGE OUR PARENTS LEFT US

Experiences of racial trauma rarely start in our lifetime, so it is helpful to look at the generations that precede us. When we explore the traumatic experiences of our forebears, in a country that was overtly hostile and violent toward them because of their Blackness, we can be struck by the apparent lack of emotional response from them. They were surrounded by reminders that they did not belong. "No Irish, no Blacks, no dogs" and "No coloureds" come to mind, along with similar notices placed on shop doors or property ads that marked them, without a shadow of a doubt, as Other.

The invisibilization of their stories of racism, bolstered by narratives of strength and resilience, masks what might be happening intergenerationally. Similarly, in the colonial context, many of us have been told about the mundane acts of humiliation and banal degradation our parents and grandparents had to endure. Stories of everyday, normalized dehumanization that came with racial oppression. Stories of being required to bow one's head before white people. Stories of being whipped in white Christian missionary schools. Stories of being spat at.

One account from my stepfather has stayed with me. It is the story of a white manager in Brazzaville disciplining a Black employee by asking him to open his mouth, spitting in the gaping orifice, then asking the Black man to swallow the phlegm. A perfect allegory, I have always thought, for colonialism. Revisiting these stories, the apparent "lack" of emotional suffering raises alarms. Coping or defense mechanisms such as dissociating from trauma in order to survive can leave children burdened with the trauma their parents never processed.

A reminder: trauma knows no time boundary. Underestimating the consequences of trauma may result in subsequent generations being more vulnerable than their forebears. Offspring may not be aware that they are carrying and experiencing, at least in part, the trauma of their parents and forebears. A multilevel understanding of racial trauma reminds us that some of the distress we may experience is not only due to what is happening to us in the "here and now." It could also be caused by what happened in the "there and then" such as the treatment of previous generations through historical atrocities, discrimination, cultural oppression, and associated unprocessed wounds. Wounds that are not allowed to heal since their scabs are constantly being removed in white supremacy. The past and the present shape how we experience the world and how our mental health is impacted by the world around us.

Intergenerational trauma is grossly neglected in psychological and mental health practice in the UK. This absence makes little sense. If, as we will see later in the book, silence is often a consequence of trauma, then this institutional silence may well be evidence of its presence. Conceptualizations of trauma are mainly highly individualistic and centered on the psychological consequences of exposure to adverse events on single individuals. When we think about trauma at a collective level, however, we tend to think about the way entire groups of people are harmed by a single event or process or how their collective identity shifts as a result of events they may not themselves have directly experienced or witnessed.[24] It is still not exactly clear how wounds are passed on from generation to generation, but various theories exist.

For instance, Shelly Harrell, whose six-part racial trauma framework we saw earlier, argues that storytelling that focuses on the hardship of those who came before us is one way to pass on trauma. So is the sharing of past survival strategies or coping mechanisms, such as being taught to put your head down and work twice as hard, being encouraged to not trust white people, and so on. Trauma may be transferred culturally by entire societies. Another African American scholar, Joy DeGruy, has theorized the existence of a **Post Traumatic Slave**

Syndrome (PTSS) as a form of trauma experienced by the descendants of enslaved Africans, resulting from centuries of racial oppression and associated survival strategies transferred through the generations. DeGruy believes that PTSS can lead to "dysfunction" interpersonally, emotionally, and behaviorally. This dysfunction may look like uncontained anger, self-neglect, and difficulties with intimacy.

Unconscious communication such as psychological projection, which is when our thoughts, feelings, and fantasies are communicated nonverbally to those around us, is also believed to be a way of passing down intergenerational trauma.[25] Think about how terror-filled gazes from one's parents can allow for powerful messages about the world to be passed on to a child. Increasingly it is also believed that biological mechanisms (e.g., epigenetics) may be conduits to pass on such trauma.[26]

Epigenetics could be described as the intersection between nature, or the genes we have inherited, and nurture, or life experiences or history of trauma. Adverse events and trauma can in some circumstances change the way DNA is expressed, and these changes can also be passed on to subsequent generations.[27] They can affect how we react to stress and adapt to various environments, our vulnerability to certain illnesses, and even our mortality.

The picture of biological transmission is still unclear and disputed, but researchers are trying to elucidate the mechanisms that may be involved; epigenetics is a relatively new area. Still, evidence of some transmission of harm can be found. In many cases, the children and grandchildren of trauma survivors, especially the offspring of those who experienced genocidal violence, are at increased risk of psychological distress.[28] Although most of these studies have focused on the descendants of Holocaust survivors, we know that in the UK, for example, children of Black migrants tend to experience more psychological distress than both their parents and their white counterparts.[29] Research has demonstrated that, in the US, psychological distress appears higher too in the children of those who survived the civil rights struggle. This suggests a similar generational pattern despite the difference in circumstances. There are, of course, various factors that account for that increased level of distress in second- and third-generation migrants and the descendants of mass trauma survivors. But the unaddressed trauma of previous generations and the conspiracies of silence around it are increasingly believed to be part of the picture.

TRAUMA AND THE BRAIN

We have known for a while that adverse experiences can fundamentally affect how our brain functions and how we experience the world. So, we can borrow from this extensive **neuroscience** literature to understand some of the challenges some may experience as a result of racism. Bessel van der Kolk, a psychiatrist and leading expert on trauma and PTSD, argues that there are three major ways that the brain can change as a response to trauma:

1. **Our fear center may become oversensitive.** This may translate into us becoming overwhelmed when we perceive situations as threatening. In other words, one of the oldest and most "primitive" parts of the brain responds more easily to fear, which is why van der Kolk refers to traumatized brains as "fear-driven brains."

2. **Our ability to filter out what is relevant from what isn't may be compromised.** This makes it difficult to stay in the present as our attention is frequently divided and takes us either into the past or into an imagined fearful future.

3. **The part of the brain responsible for how we experience the world can change.** As a result, many trauma survivors can find it incredibly difficult to have a strong sense of who they are post-trauma.[30]

Although these changes may not affect all of us, a closer look at neuroscience can help us better make sense of these common experiences and perhaps of some of the challenges we may experience.

Four cerebral systems responsible for processing information and managing threats can change with trauma:

1. The **hippocampus**

   The hippocampus plays a major role in learning and memory. People with histories of trauma often have abnormalities in this brain region. The hippocampus contributes to us recording new memories and retrieving them later in response to specific stimuli or events in our environment. The hippocampus also helps us distinguish between past and present. We can now better understand why feeling triggered or feeling taken back is a common experience in trauma survivors.

2. The **amygdala**

   The amygdala's primary role is the management of our emotional responses or emotional regulation; this includes the management of fear, anxiety and aggression. The amygdala is so implicated in the survival response that it is sometimes thought of as a threat or danger alarm. So, the amygdala is central to how we respond to situations that remind us of or resemble past traumatic events. Trauma appears to increase activity in the amygdala, rendering it hypersensitive. This helps explain why trauma survivors are sensitive to distress caused by fear and anxiety and why they so often struggle with feeling safe.

3. The **prefrontal cortex**

   The prefrontal cortex is central to the more sophisticated and complex cognitive functions such as planning, analyzing, or strategizing, capacities sometimes referred to as the "executive functions." Those who have experienced significant trauma can show changes in that brain region. The prefrontal cortex is also responsible for our conscious ability to inhibit the amygdala and to manage our fears. Hence, trauma survivors often experience difficulties with thinking, memory, and/or concentration, and this may be why it can be harder to manage our emotions after significant trauma.

4. **Autonomic nervous system**

The autonomic nervous system has been compared to a control system that regulates several bodily functions, including threat-based bodily responses such as increased heart and respiratory rates. The autonomous nervous system controls our fight-or-flight response and our response to stressors. When we have repeatedly been exposed to acute or chronic stress it becomes much more difficult for us to regulate our autonomic nervous system. This can explain why we may feel we have little control over our body.[31]

HEALING TRAUMA

As we have seen, it is partly because of the changes in the brain that follow trauma that we can experience difficulties in managing fear and stress.[32] It can be why some of us may really struggle to feel safe in the world. It may be why we experience the kind of difficulties van der Kolk says are so common in trauma survivors. British clinical psychologist Paul Gilbert created the **compassion-focused therapy (CFT)** model to redress these difficulties. He also suggests that trauma and other adverse experiences such as abuse or neglect often result in individuals developing high levels of shame, self-criticalness, and hostility toward themselves; for example, by being harsh or punishing themselves when they make mistakes.

In other words, for those with a history of trauma, the brain "soothing system" or the capacity to self-reassure is not easily accessible and believed to be underdeveloped. This can cause some of us to have difficulties experiencing sanctuary and safeness because the neural systems that activate these feelings are thought to have been underused. Instead, self-criticalness and hostility become the way to manage emotions. This further reduces the capacity to feel safe, soothed, and reassured, and repeats histories of poor treatment. This is important.

The compassion-focused therapy framework essentially suggests that we can increase our sense of unsafety by treating ourselves harshly. The idea is that the brain is not able to tell the difference between psychological threats (e.g., racial name calling) and physical threats (e.g., someone chasing us with a knife). Crucially, our brain also cannot tell the difference between external threats, what comes from the social world (e.g., racial discrimination), and what comes from within (e.g., self-hate). Our brain responds the same way in all cases, triggering fear in our threat center and our fight-or-flight response via complex hormonal and neurobiological events. The impact of trauma on the brain does not have to be a life sentence. Our brains are not immutable and continue to grow and change throughout life. Reparative experiences and relevant mindful deliberate action following trauma can fundamentally alter our brain structure too. The idea that experiences can shape our cerebral environment and brain structures is referred to as **neuroplasticity**.[33] And so, we can heal from trauma. In the context of white supremacy, healing must be deliberate, targeted, and a lifelong process. Our first task is to do what we can to counteract external and internal threats.

Encouragingly, there are steps we can take to help ensure we do not unnecessarily create unsafeness for ourselves, and we can learn to practice self-soothing and relaxation to counteract what racism may have caused. In the following chapters, these strategies will be explored.[34]

SUMMARY

1.

Black people continue to be poorly served in white institutions. In this chapter, we considered racial inequalities within the mental health system and their consequences for Black people.

2.

Racial trauma, which as a framework aims to make visible the harm of racism, must be considered beyond the individual. The intergenerational transmission of trauma that may take place via various mechanisms likely contributes to the excess of psychological distress in Black groups.

3.

Our brain can change as a result of trauma and adverse experiences. Such changes can result in us having difficulties feeling soothed and safe and in us becoming prone to shame, which in turn can compromise our sense of safety in the world.

4.

Adverse experiences and trauma can fundamentally alter how we process information, relate to the world, and relate to ourselves. It is thus important that we understand the basic neurobiology of trauma so we may understand why our bodies and minds respond in the way they do and understand what may help reverse the damage of racism.

....

In the next chapter, "Black Shame," we examine the psychological world of Blackness and consider the specific ways in which racism can enter our minds and harm our mental health.

RACE REFLECTIONS

You have explored the institutional context of Black mental health and the impact of the past on our contemporary experiences of racism. This section gives you the opportunity to reflect and develop skills to help resist and help protect your mental health from racism.

What did you find most challenging in this chapter?
You may want to explore the images, thoughts, and physical responses that came to you and explore what they might take you back to. Please use the Race Reflections reflective model (p. 183) to help you. _____ _____ _____ _____ _____

It is impossible to understand Black mental health without understanding the impact of historical trauma.
When it comes to your history, what events have shaped your experience of the world? _____ _____ _____ _____ _____

Current definitions of mental health problems may not necessarily
reflect the challenges we face in the world. Still, it is important to think
about what keeps us well and actively seek to stay well.

*What is mental health to you? What does being well look like to you? Think
about ways you can incorporate social justice and community building in
your definition.*

_____

_____

_____

_____

_____

For various reasons, seeking help can be difficult for many of us.
Accepting that we, like anyone else, are deserving of support and care
humanizes us, as does connecting with the community around us.
Tapping into community and social support also acts
as a protective factor.

*Who forms your support network? Who can you call on if distressed? What
may you need to do to sustain and nurture relationships with people in
your network?*

_____

_____

_____

_____

_____

ACTION POINT
PRACTICE GRATITUDE

Trauma makes us sensitive to possible threats in our environment. This focus on or disposition to notice things that are threatening and painful can contribute to emotional distress and keep our internal world out of balance. We need to be conscious and deliberate in paying attention to the little things that make life worth living, the things we are grateful for amid the injustice. Furthermore, practicing gratitude is linked to better well-being.

Your action point: Commit to recording in your journal at least one thing (and up to three) for which you are grateful, every day.

It could be something as simple as the sun on your skin on a particularly glorious day, an act of kindness toward you, the smile or comfort a friend or child gave to you, a good laugh, or a good read. Practicing gratitude is a helpful way to rebalance our attention and connect differently to the world.

CHAPTER 3

BLACK SHAME

What does it really feel like to live in a society that repeatedly tells you that you are not welcome and that you do not belong? This chapter explores these questions.

Extraordinarily little has been written about the lived experience and psychological impact of racism. In this chapter we delve into the ways in which racism enters our mind and body and wreaks havoc with our internal worlds, generation after generation. We also look at why so many of us are likely to, at some point in our life, experience psychological distress. To do this we will consider shame, injustice, and homelessness as central elements in Black people's experiences of the world and examine their impact on our psychological functioning.

INTERSECTIONALITY AND TRAUMA

Case study: Fiona

Fiona, a fifty-five-year-old woman of mixed heritage, has seen both her parents being racially abused. In particular, as a young child she witnessed her Black father being chased by a racist mob. Fiona's mother, a white migrant, could not cope with the racism. The family unit disintegrated. Fiona was taken into care. In care, Fiona's cultural needs as a mixed-race child were erased. She was regularly racially harassed, to the point that she attempted to rub the Blackness out of her skin with scrubbing pads and bleach. Fiona reported experiencing racism often at the hands of the police. She was also sexually abused in care, and when she tried to speak of her abuse to social services she was not believed. Fiona also shared some of her experiences as an adult. Once, when she confronted a neighbor who had racially harassed her, the police were called and went on to arrest Fiona. The racial components of the dispute and its response were ignored. Fiona's complaints were dismissed. Fiona described an incident she faced, much later in life, during her studies: within a child observation class, a "mixed-race" child was described as "Mediterranean" by a fellow student who was white. Her attempts at exploring what she considered to be an act of "subtle middle-class racism" were ignored. Fiona described how for a year after this event, she went on to have nightmares in which she was beating up the student who had erased the Blackness of the child.

Fiona's trauma is complex and centered around racism. Racism was the main cause for the distress her mother experienced, the catalyst for the family separation, the reason for the self-hatred Fiona experienced, and the source of her having her cultural identity erased. In addition to racial abuse, Fiona suffered sexual abuse, which is also instrumental to her vulnerability and trauma history. Acts of racial injustice may have amplified or triggered memories of interpersonal trauma such as Fiona's sexual abuse, leading to the reproduction of messages of inferiority.

Fiona's unexpressed rage at her violent gendered and racialized objectification manifested in those nightmares. One may argue that these nightmares are an act of displacement of the repressed anger she may feel toward whiteness and/or her white mother, both of which may have come to symbolize abandonment, dismissal, and erasure. There are parallels between her initial experience of being silenced about her sexual abuse and the way her experience of racism has been consistently denied in various social structures, such as the police and mental health services. Fiona spoke to me about her body and her belief that racism contributed to her getting breast cancer. (In chapter 4, we will look at the impact of racism on the body.)

UNDERSTANDING INTERSECTIONALITY

Experiences of racial injustice and racism are inextricably linked to other, non-race-related experiences of injustice, trauma, and other axes of oppression. Black American law professor and feminist Kimberlé Crenshaw coined the term "**intersectionality**" to conceptualize how combined systems of oppression (based on gender, race, sexuality, class, age, religion, and disability) are interconnected.[1] They lead to varying experiences and vulnerability to subordination and discrimination. Research on this is starting to emerge. Large-scale statistical analyses have shown that the number of marginalized groups and the frequency of discrimination have more explanatory power when it comes to measuring risk of developing PTSD than when considering contextual factors alone. Those who have experienced more adversities in life tend to be more distressed when faced with racism and racial injustice. Therefore, intersectional lenses are required to make sense of Black people's experiences and the nuances of anti-Blackness.

More widely, people affected by racial trauma often have non-racism-related trauma histories. I have worked with individuals who after being exposed to racism-related abuses started to have flashbacks of childhood experiences of sexual abuse. In my own research, participants who had experienced more interpersonal trauma, such as being separated from parents as children and/or being bullied, appeared to experience more distress when faced with racial injustice. I have thus argued that racial trauma intersects with other experiences of injustice and trauma. Research on gendered racism has found that multiple oppressions are generally associated with increased psychological distress.[2]

MORE ON SHAME

As we have seen in chapter 2, all trauma survivors must contend with shame.

When it comes to Blackness, from the treatment of our ancestors to enduring race inequalities and racial hostility, we are deeply affected and shaped by racial injustice and what happened in the past, and this includes the violence and shame our forebears experienced. Shame results in low self-worth, identification with those who harm us, silence, and suppressed feelings. Shame, including malignant shame, is equally transmissible. Oppressed groups, including Black people, are governed by shame, and in turn we learn to navigate the world through shame. The cycles of shame-based abuse and self-relating or self-policing are transmitted into the future.

Shame exists at various levels. The late French West Indian psychiatrist and postcolonial author Frantz Fanon, in *Black Skin, White Masks*, eloquently described how colonialism has distorted Black people's understanding of their Blackness, as we come to internalize white colonizers' gaze and racist constructions of savagery, inferiority, and deficiency.[3] These constructions continue to lead to deep feelings of shame and self-hatred, which many of us attempt to reconcile by rejecting aspects of our Blackness. The politics of **assimilation** and of **respectability** speak of this shame. They are therefore based on self-hate. Although they may provide temporary escape and possibly material gain and conditional access to structures of power, they reproduce white supremacy and as such breed further shame and self-alienation. Self-contempt, disdain, and scorn were not merely accidental by-products of colonialism—they were manufactured, deliberate colonial weapons to fortify whiteness and reduce resistance. But the toxic shame we are talking about is not only a colonial residue, nor is it only related to race and racism.

When we are harmed systematically and repeatedly, eventually we start to believe that we deserve that which is done to us. It follows in our thinking that there is something deeply broken and dysfunctional about us. Trauma survivors often adopt these beliefs. **Patriarchy** offers an alternative and intersecting system of subjugation upon which this reality can be observed, often across a range of traumas. For instance, physically and sexually abused women tend to feel a deep sense of shame over their abuse. Male, cisgender perpetrators of gendered violence clearly benefit from women or their victims experiencing shame, not least because it reduces the possibility of accountability. In fact, it shifts accountability altogether by silently encouraging women to self-blame and self-hate for the sexual violence they have experienced, rendering them much less likely to speak out and seek justice.

Similarly, the myth of meritocracy is reproduced when poor and socially disadvantaged groups feel shame for not achieving the social "success" of their more privileged counterparts.[4] When inadequacy rather than unjust disadvantage is internalized as an explanatory model, it is less likely that unfair structures will be dismantled. Shame takes hold and devours the will to resist and dissent. The impact of racism on Black bodies and minds is partly mediated by introjected shame so that each spit, insult, microaggression, and act of exclusion reminds us that we are Other. That somehow we are responsible. We are to blame. This leads naturally to intensified and chronic distress, distress that is often unaddressed because it is also subject to shame.

Since we are supposed to be both inhuman and superhuman, or inhuman because we are superhuman, when these internalized notions of Black strength, resilience, and invulnerability do not match our lived reality we may feel inadequate.[5] This further increases our distress and provides additional evidence that we are not enough. As there are also shame and stigma around mental health difficulties in our communities, some of this stigma is independent from the mental health inequalities encountered in chapter 1. We are much less likely to seek help and instead may opt to suffer in silence and in shame. That shame and stigma cannot be separated from long-standing association between Blackness and madness, Blackness and psychological or intellectual inferiority, and related cultural inheritances.

Shame is not only used by abusers to manipulate our emotions. Often it also functions as a compass to evaluate our worth or as evidence of our lack of the same. As a result, when we experience shame, we may become fearful that speaking of it may lead others to evaluate us in the way we evaluate ourselves. To know we are worthless rather than to know that we *feel* worthless. Basically, to be found out. Perhaps this helps explain why shame can be difficult to own up to and speak about.[6]

THE IMPACT OF INJUSTICE

As Black people, there is no single part of our existence that has not been touched by injustice—directly or indirectly. I do not consider the events laid out in this book to be unusual. Nor do I consider myself or the people who come to see me for support to be outliers when it comes to our experience of racism. As mentioned in chapter 1, there is something dysfunctional in how we define psychological dysfunction or in how we define mental health problems.[7] I tend to think of mental health problems as acts of resistance to injustice that sometimes have undesired or unintended effects. The erasure of the impact of injustice in mental health frameworks is another failing that serves whiteness. There is nothing pathological in being hurt and destabilized by injustice in the world. It is what makes us human. There is no glory in adapting to injustice and inhumanity, contrary to what mental health practices often tell us. Each time we socialize ourselves into accepting injustice we cut ourselves off from parts of our humanity. We normalize social inequality and add a layer of protection to an already solid status quo.

The lived experience of injustice is central to the excess of psychological distress we experience. I have long proposed that it leads to a form of **ontological insecurity**: chronic feelings of unsafeness and detachment in the world. When we face injustice and we recognize it as such, our self-image often shifts. Our relationships with the world and with ourselves are often affected.[8] Our sense of belonging and being in the world can become shaky. Our world is transformed. I believe the need for justice is anchored deeply within us. Through our lived experience of racial injustice, social inequalities become internal events; they take hold and lodge themselves in our bodies. It is not coincidental that the experiences that most accurately predict psychological distress, such as bullying, discrimination, sexual abuse, poverty, and even bereavement seem to all involve a breached sense of justice. This breach of the principle or expectation of justice seems to profoundly distress us.

Reflecting on my own clinical work, I do not believe that I have ever met a single person in distress who was not struggling with injustice one way or the other: From the persecuted asylum seeker who feels God's fury has turned on them despite devoting their entire life to religion to the child who cannot comprehend why they are the one being picked on at school for being "different." From the parents struggling to say good-bye to a dying child to those who have been laid off because of ageism or sexism or those whose body was objectified in the most degrading ways. Injustice turns us into robots. Injustice causes despair. Injustice wounds us deeply. No amount of psychological support can ever help an entire group thrive without addressing unjust social structures and racial injustice.[9]

WHAT WE CALL HOME

Case study: Eileen

Eileen (pronouns: they/their) is a nonbinary Black patient I spoke with as part of my research. Eileen was admitted to a hospital in London with suspected multiple sclerosis. Once there, they quickly noticed they were treated differently from white patients. They told me that during the rounds when they got to their bed, the way in which staff would address them was completely different from how they addressed everyone else. Other patients might get a "good morning," while they would get a "so, we are looking at your file," and there wouldn't even be a greeting. When they were acknowledged, their body was handled with contempt or hostility. They felt manhandled and as though there were little regard for the discomfort they were caused. Convinced these experiences in the hospital ward were due to their Blackness, they made complaints, which were dismissed. They returned home. Their health deteriorated. They started to urinate blood and then became blind in one eye. They did not seek support for several weeks, remaining in pain and at home. When I asked them why they had not sought help, they said they could no longer be sure they could trust their body, due to being told so many times that they were wrong in their experience. The impact of repeated experience of denial had altered Eileen's relationship with their body and with reality. How many of us have come to doubt our own reality when it is denied in situations of racism?

DENIAL, SHAME, AND INJUSTICE

The denial of racism can have serious consequences. Denial is part of the cycle of abuse. Some researchers have conceptualized it as secondary injury akin to "rubbing toxins into an open wound." Silencing or denial significantly increase distress after initial racist incidents. Yet covert or subtle racism makes it virtually impossible to objectively establish the occurrence or nonoccurrence of racism beyond the **embodied** experiences of the person on the receiving end of it, lending it particularly well to that process of internal displacement. An uprooting of marginalized people from their internal home due to chronic **gaslighting** when they attempt to speak of their experience of the world is enacted through the misuse of power. Is it any wonder that so many Black people are vulnerable to diagnoses of psychosis, or become dissociated from their own reality like Eileen, when the home that is their sense of truth and reality is chronically rendered precarious? This is what I have referred to as **epistemic homelessness**. I argue that our capacity to know is dependent on our capacity to have a home.

In 2017, in preparation for my TEDx Talk on the subject, I ran a few polls on social media, asking three questions. First, I asked whether people of color found covert or overt racism more challenging. Based on responses of the 549 people who answered, covert racism was found to be about seven times more challenging. Second, I asked about the outcome of conversations about subtle discrimination. The results were that a whopping 95 percent said they were mocked, ignored, or not believed when they named their experience of subtle racism. Finally, I inquired about the impact of such invalidation. The most common feeling reported was that one was "losing one's mind," which was experienced by 36 percent of participants, followed by 32 percent saying that they felt pain or were in distress. Other reported feelings included rage, helplessness, exhaustion, shame, disbelief, and the sense of being gaslighted.

These findings are consistent with my own clinical experience and with other research findings on the serious psychological impact of **microaggressions**. The term "racial microaggressions" was coined by African American psychiatrist Chester Pierce to describe everyday and often subtle insults, indignities, and dismissals experienced by Americans of color and which affected their mental health.[10] Experiences of covert bigotry often create much more race-based distress than more overt and direct expressions of racism. Not only are the triggering effects of strategically ambiguous words or deeds often loaded with racial denigration; Black targets are often left to do hours of cognitive work. Hours of hypothesis testing. Hours of rumination. Hours replaying, often second by second, what was said or what was done, in the hope of trusting that they know what they do indeed know. Gaslighting ourselves and, in doing so, reproducing the contempt this society holds toward our capacity to know and our authority.

SHAKY HOMES, SHAKY ATTACHMENTS

We traditionally speak of attachment to focus on the infant-caregiver bond and its long-lasting impact on how we come to experience relationships and the world.[11] Outside of mental health disciplines, others have interrogated the importance of place in terms of human functioning and orientation. Increasingly, there is scrutiny of the emotional bonds or attachments that exist between locations and people.

"**Place attachment**" refers to the strong emotional bond we develop with a specific location.[12] Like infant-caregiver attachments, our relationship with places is reciprocal and shaped by how we are responded to as well as by the nature of our experiences. Place attachment is thought to be composed of two intersecting dimensions: a sense of rootedness and of sense of place. Rootedness is related to history, ancestry, and lineage. It is the sense of familiarity that arises with habitual residence over time. Sense of place, on the other hand, is more subjective. It is to do with meaning-making, the symbolic connections and internal narratives we make and maintain about locations. Place attachment helps us to think about and make sense of our relationship with the world.

Homeness, homelessness, and belonging are central themes in Black groups' experiences of psychological distress.[13] Through our history of displacement and immigration, homelessness has huge significance. As a result of the transatlantic slave trade, many of us have been born far from our ultimate ancestral lands. This disconnection already renders home-making complex. In addition, our sense of homeness is rendered precarious by immigration and associated racism and xenophobia. It is tough to feel secure in one's home when your skin forever marks you as an outsider. As not belonging. As not really from "here," especially when the threat of dispossession or deportation always looms. Racism compromises cultural affiliation and the sense of home. How can your home be truly your home if entry into it and your right of abode is conditional? When this right can so easily be denied under the racist fantasy that some other home will always be yours for you to claim and return to. Even when that connection barely exists. Even if that presumed home is in fact much more unfamiliar than your usual place of dwelling.[14]

WINDRUSH AND THE HOSTILE ENVIRONMENT

In the United Kingdom, "the hostile environment" refers to successive sets of policies and legislative measures, implemented by the Home Office, specifically designed to render the UK hostile and inhospitable for those migrants it deemed to have no legal right to remain in the UK.[15] The bulk of the hostile environment measures came into action with the Immigration Act 2014 and have since been expanded under subsequent legislation. In everyday terms, "the hostile environment" meant the state making it as hard as possible for migrants to work, to find housing, to access healthcare, and to open bank accounts. And of course, since whiteness belongs and Blackness does not, those with Black skin, the forever aliens of the land, were disproportionately impacted. The Windrush atrocity provides an illustration of the racialization of "home."

The term "Windrush Generation" refers to those people from the Caribbean who came to the UK between 1948 and 1973, invited to fill Britain's postwar labor shortage and help rebuild the nation. The name "Windrush" originates from the HMT *Empire Windrush* ship, which carried one of the largest and earliest groups in 1948. Because the Caribbean was, at the time, a part of the British Commonwealth, those who arrived were automatically British subjects and free to permanently live and work in the UK. Still, these citizens were required to "prove" decades later their right to live in the UK through draconian and inhuman processes that resulted in hundreds unable to document their status. In addition, the Home Office reportedly destroyed the records of many.

As a result, many were deported, and families were broken; parents, children, and siblings separated; loving partners torn apart; and generations of relatives traumatized by a British immigration system apparently set on inflicting violence on those whose bodies it deemed no longer of value. Bodies who had a right to be in the UK all along. Bodies that were deemed expendable and could therefore be subjected to bureaucratic degradation and routine humiliation. It left many ill, distraught, and suicidal. At least eleven of the wrongly deported died. Numbers are disputed. Disputed but, of course, not tracked.

At the time of this writing, and despite the government issuing an apology, most Windrush survivors have yet to receive the support and compensation promised to them. It is hard to miss that those displaced from their land and shipped to the other end of the world were once more being treated like disposable cargo shippable to "the Americas."[16] The trauma of such border violence, combined with a history of separation and displacement, is severe. Although it hit right in the heart of people of Caribbean heritage, subsequent waves of people from the Commonwealth at large have also been affected by the hostile environment and faced degradation, deportation, and violence. The context of forced "migration" for US Black populations has also left an indelible stain on the collective sense of homelessness and disconnection—experiences compounded upon contemporary experiences of Othering and notions that the US is not Black Americans' "real" home.

With forced "migration" comes dislocation. Individuals and groups are extracted from their homes and from what they know. This displacement shifts how we experience ourselves and our identity. It disrupts the sense of the familiar. Roots and cultural bearings lose their proximity. Family and friends often fade into memories, often bloody memories. This sense of loss and disconnection can be profound and can last for generations, affecting those displaced, their children, and those who come after. It is no coincidence that displacement is associated with psychological distress and poor mental health.[17] Feeling disconnected causes psychological distress. Psychological distress in turn causes further disconnection.

A framework that has been developed to describe the ongoing struggle to find a home among those whose identities sit at the crossroad of two or more cultures is that of **cultural homelessness**.[18] We are said to feel culturally homeless when we do not feel quite at home in the mainstream culture and at the same time feel disconnected from our ancestry and heritage. Often, this is due to repeated experiences of marginalization, discrimination, or exclusion in one or both cultures. It is the sense of not feeling quite at home anywhere that leads Black Americans to seek ties with Africa and that has been central to the quest for Pan-Africanism. Cultural homelessness can leave us feeling vulnerable, unprotected, and forever in search of a sense of belonging. This cultural alienation and yearning are part of the puzzle of mental health inequalities.

Finally, there is another level of homelessness that we barely speak about honestly, related to the story of alleged Black betrayal, the ultimate "Black on Black violence," some say. It is unspoken mainly because of the trauma and shame around it. This is one of the most painful Black conversations. Growing up, it was a constant presence in my relationship with people of Caribbean heritage. It carried centuries of pain and unhealed wounds that exist across the diaspora.

These notions are rooted in anti-Blackness. No one says of World War I or World War II that they started because white people started to kill other white people. No one takes them as illustrations of "white on white violence." It is a reality that conflicts tend to occur between those who are in proximity. And throughout history there have always been collaborators in situations of war, conflict, and oppression. Black history and the history of the transatlantic slave trade is no different. It is absolutely true, without a shadow of a doubt, that there were African collaborators who, out of fear, coercion, or for material gain, supported

the slave trade. Slave catchers who were Africans, kings who sold pris-
oners from enemy tribes to Europeans. But there were also millions of
people resisting and fighting slavers. This history has not reached the
stories we tell ourselves, and this is not a coincidence. The systematic
destruction of colonial and imperial documents and the retelling of
our history through the white gaze and its associated "recollections"
and distortions has resulted in the widespread erasure of this reality.
Carrying the belief consciously or otherwise that your ancestors were
sold while there was no attempt to resist, to stop them from leaving
the shores of Africa, that even your ancestors sought to get rid of you,
leaves you vulnerable to feeling unwanted. The sense of homelessness
is reproduced at ancestral levels. We must therefore add nuance to this
story and remember the impact of such historical lies and half-truths.

SUMMARY

1.

Experiences of shame, injustice, and homelessness are central to the psychological distress of Black people. These considerations are often absent from conversations on mental health.

2.

When considering responses to racism it is vital that we consider other experiences of trauma, adverse life experiences, and other axes of oppression. This is what I refer to as the intersection of trauma.

3.

Injustices may leave an imprint on the soul, which fundamentally shifts our relationship with our self, our body, and the world. But every system relies on those it harms believing they deserve the harm and violence aimed at them.

4.

Externalizing this belief alone would do so much for our collective mental health. Externalizing this belief is therefore a matter of public health.

....

The next chapter, "Black Bodies," discusses the physical consequences of racism and explores the physical demands and violence carried out on Black people.

RACE REFLECTIONS

Shame, injustice, and homelessness are specific ways we may come to be harmed by racism. This section gives you the opportunity to reflect and develop skills to resist and protect your mind from racism.

What was the most challenging aspect of this chapter for you?

You may want to explore the images, thoughts, and physical responses that came to you and explore what they might take you back to. Please use the Race Reflections reflective model (p. 183) to help you.

_____

_____

_____

_____

_____

Shame is a powerful emotion that often accompanies trauma.

You are invited to reflect on your experiences of shame. What brings on feelings of shame in you? What do you tend to do when you feel ashamed? Where might you have learned to respond in this way, and what are the pros and cons of this response?

_____

_____

_____

_____

_____

We have learned the centrality of injustice in our experience of the world.

What is your relationship to injustice? How do you tend to respond when you witness injustice or are treated unjustly? How do your reactions relate to your previous experience of injustice? What helps you get a sense of justice?

_____

_____

_____

_____

_____

We are often shaped by our caregivers' or our parents' experiences of the world even when these experiences appear not to have affected them.

What significant life events have your parents experienced that might have shaped their worldview and the messages they have communicated to you about the world?

_____

_____

_____

_____

_____

ACTION POINT

STRENGTHEN HOMENESS

Your action point: Before you complete *Living While Black* you are invited to increase your sense of homeness. Think about your home in as many contexts as you can, such as your physical home, your cultural home, and your epistemic home, and take steps to make each of these homes as comfortable and safe as you can.

In terms of your physical home, can you think of ways to make it feel more welcoming and safe for you? If you don't have an entire house, can you make your room as comfortable as possible? What could you do to want to spend more time in this space? To make it feel more secure and homely? In terms of your cultural home, how many cultural homes do you have? Some actions can increase our sense of connection to a culture, such as learning and speaking the language and regularly visiting and/or learning about the place's history.

For your "epistemic" home, learn to trust your experience and your body, your beliefs, the ways your body lets you know what is real or what is not. Your body and mind primarily exist to keep you safe. How might you remind yourself of this?

CHAPTER 4

BLACK BODIES

You go into a room. It is a white space.

As you enter, you feel a sense of heaviness. You look around and notice pairs of eyes staring as though devouring you. You instantly realize you are the only person of color in the space. A sort of malaise takes hold of you. You feel a little queasy. Perhaps the discomfort starts to make you feel dizzy. You may experience nausea. You might attempt to stick around and impose your presence, in silence. You may even take a seat, but, in any case, your body is reacting to something. Soon enough that something becomes overwhelming. Every move you make is with microscopic precision, as self-consciousness takes over your body. Your Blackness is in sharp closeup from the outside in. You know you want to exit now. You know this space is inhospitable to you. It may start to feel hard to breathe, and so you try to look for a way out and a reason to leave discreetly. You find one, and you disappear almost as quickly as you entered. Your departure likely goes unnoticed. What happened in that room? What was your body reacting to? Is this only anxiety, or have you been expelled from that space? Whose fantasy were you acting out?[1]

This chapter centers on the Black body—the Black body as a site of violence but also the Black body as a site of contestation. The impact of racism is often lodged in the Black body. So, in this chapter, in order to further our understanding of racial trauma on Black groups, we examine how Black bodies become permeated by whiteness, how they are transformed and shaped by white supremacy, and how the impact of racist violence, even when only psychological, affects our physical health.

The above scenario illustrates how quickly and covertly we can be policed and consumed. How powerfully yet invisibly we can be excluded. It is a painful reminder that in the white imagination there are still so few spaces we can rightfully claim as ours. Furthermore, I have no doubt that, to most Black readers, walking into a hostile white space will be known, if not cognitively, then through their body. Most of us have been taught to discount knowledge that we acquire through our body, our embodied experience of the world. Partly this is due to whiteness and its hyper-rational aspirations. Partly this is because as Black people we have been taught to replace our subjectivity or our experience of the world with that of those who do us harm. This is partly a survival strategy, but it is intergenerational trauma too. So, we learn to be suspicious of our senses and ignore what our body tells us about that world, in the same way, again, as ancestral and indigenous traditions were erased through colonialism.

BLACK BODIES, WHITE FANTASIES

I started this chapter by using an expression many will find controversial. Many may feel that using the term "Black bodies" is dehumanizing. But I use "body" rather than "person" for more than one reason. First, it emphasizes the fact that we are racialized as Black because of the characteristics of our bodies. Second, the term stresses that the violence done to us is often done to our bodies. Our bodies, but not necessarily our personhood, therefore, are sites of racial violence.

There is a long history of emphasizing the politics of the body within social justice and critical scholarship. But to challenge Cartesian thought, which splits bodily experiences from the intellectual domain, I also seek to honor the knowledge we gather from our body, or what I refer to as "embodied data." Finally, and this is a point that American Jamaican poet and playwright Claudia Rankine makes: our bodies arouse fantasies in the white mind that rob us of our personhood. It is the image of Blackness that is seen, and that image of Blackness is not that of a sibling; it is not that of a child or a friend. It is a Black body that needs restraining, containing, or neutralizing. Rankine says, "When white men are shooting Black people, some of it is malice and some an out-of-control image of Blackness in their minds. Darren Wilson told the jury that he shot Michael Brown because he looked like a demon. And I do not disbelieve it. Blackness in the white imagination has nothing to do with Black people."[2] Rankine refers to the grotesque killing that took place on August 9, 2014, in Ferguson, Missouri. Brown was just eighteen when he was killed by Officer Wilson, who was twenty-eight.

The story starts with Brown and his friend Dorian Johnson leaving a convenience store and ends with him being shot twelve times. The final shot was in the head. Facts remain contested, and, of course, Brown took his side of the story to the grave. At the crime scene, Brown's body was left to lie on the street for four and a half hours. In court, Wilson described Brown as though he were a monster, an out-of-control wild animal full of rage, aggressive, hostile, "crazy," and threatening his life. He described him as a "demon" making a "grunting . . . aggravated sound."[3] Wilson was found not guilty, and the rest is now history.

THE WHITE GAZE

Black Skin, White Masks was the first book to examine the psychology of racism and the internalization of whiteness.[4] It also revealed the impact of white **projections** on the Black body. Racial hatred has long been thought of as a form of protection against these aspects of the self, others, or the world that white people find intolerable. Projection is a **defense mechanism** that occurs when usually unpalatable parts of the self are disowned and attributed to others.[5] Projection may be used to defend against one's sexual urges. To defend against one's immorality or sense of depravity. Or to defend against the fear of the unknown. More broadly speaking, to protect oneself against uncertainty, powerlessness, and the fear of death, some of the most primal anxieties.

Projection is therefore a way of cleansing the self by ridding it of those aspects that clash with its sense of goodness. Let's translate this into racial dynamics. In a society where often overvalued, so-called rationality is used as the only or superior way to know and access truth, the emotional and more embodied self will naturally be difficult to tolerate. The Black body therefore serves as a convenient repository of irrationality and bodily impulses. Similarly, if aggression and sexual impulses clash with white puritan or Christian constructions of innocence, chastity, and bodily mastery, then, of course, the Black body will become the carrier of sexual depravity, aggression, and impulsivity in the white imagination.

COLONIALISM: THE ONGOING
WEIGHT OF THE PAST

Our starting point to contextualize the treatment of the Black body is Western colonialism. Today it informs our Othering in white spaces, an experience that arguably unites all Black bodies on earth. As a political and socioeconomic endeavor, colonialism encompassed the exploitation and control of large areas of the world. With that came replacing colonized countries' political sovereignty with some foreign metropolitan authority or administration. Colonialism involved taking over natural resources, lands, and bodies deemed commodities. It compromised both the colonized and the colonizer's humanity.

The former ceased to exist as persons as they were stripped of everything that made them human, and the latter embodied atrocious violence and the power to possess, dispossess, and exercise brutal control. By acquiring partial or complete control over foreign regions and/ or by occupying them with settlers, colonialism was the ultimate intrusive violence, the ultimate breach of boundaries. It was rape in every sense of the word, and the boundaries breached went well beyond the geographical.

One of the ways colonialism came to be self-sustained was through the mind of the colonized. The colonizing of minds was carried out primarily by imposing racialized hierarchies topped by whiteness. This transformed the colonized sense of self and the world and led to the internalization of racist myths and constructions such as the inferiority of Black and brown people. The psychological warfare waged by co-lonialism on Black minds also included the erasure of indigenous cultures and belief systems, which created both internal and external disturbances. The long-term impact of colonialism continues to attract much attention and controversy, although there is really nothing controversial in stating that long-lasting systems of organizing every aspect of the world, including power relations, would leave some residues behind. Most of the past five hundred years have been spent with white people convinced of the intellectual inferiority of Black people, policing the Black body, ascribing it to designated territories and subservient roles, and ensuring that it did not move beyond its station. Where did all this stuff go?

There are various ways to think about the ongoing impact of the machinery of modern colonialism and how it continues to shape our existence. Postcolonialism, neocolonialism, and coloniality offer a few helpful frameworks. **Postcolonialism** is first and foremost the academic study of the legacy of colonialism and imperialism. **Neocolonialism**, a branch of postcolonial interest, deals with the way new forms of domination and subordination arose after colonized nations became "independent." It focuses on the contemporary strategies former colonial powers use to keep exploiting these countries by making them dependent, subjugated, and indebted. Finally, "coloniality" refers to the long-standing patterns of relations that emerged because of **colonialism** and continue to define our culture, power relations, intersubjective exchanges, and knowledge production. Each of these areas attract their fair bit of criticism, much of it defensive and misconceived and beyond the scope of this chapter.

One enduring line of criticism is linguistic. Some people have argued that the prefixes "neo" and "post" create the illusion of discontinuity and ending.[6] We could argue that this puts an arbitrary boundary between the present and the past. There is indeed a tendency to distance ourselves from the unpalatable by relaying it to that mythical space we call "the past," a form of dissociation that helps "us" avoid revisiting colonial atrocities and contemporary complicity. Still, relations of domination and subjugation manifest in various spaces and need to be contextualized. In many ways, as many have suggested, they are neither accidental nor incidental. Rather, they reflect the continuation of colonialism and the reproduction of the past into the present.[7]

THE BLACK BODY AND BOUNDARIES

There are various ways to understand psychological or psychic boundaries. Fundamentally, holding boundaries means separating psychological entities. It means separating our emotions, thoughts, and beliefs, or our internal world, from those of others. It can be argued that boundaries form lines that stop us from merging into others and stop others from merging into us. They consequently keep the integrity of our personhood intact. That ability to preserve our personal integrity via boundaries has been called personal sovereignty, and it concerns our capacity to protect our psychological independence, self-governance, self-determination, and freedom from unwanted authority, interference, or intrusion.

Boundaries govern how we move, how much or how little space we take up, the distance or proximity between us, the relationship between our bodies and places—all this tells us something about our sociopolitical and historical contexts. There are various ways to assert and communicate dominance and superiority, and the ways bodies move through space and are treated in space are good indicators of power relations. The interconnection between body, space, and historical racism will therefore become manifest and experienced through bodies, from the spreading of legs in public seating to subtly elbowing us out of proximity and disregarding of physical boundaries and the invisibilization of our bodies. The expectation is that the Black body gives way to the white body. I remember how once, on a busy London bus largely full of white bodies, with no seat available, an older white woman got on and went straight to a Black woman to ask her to get up. The Black body she displaced was disabled. This only became apparent when the woman got up and struggled to stand with a walking stick. A Black woman was asked to make space for a white woman amid the sea of white bodies. She was the body that was required to be displaced. This entitlement to space also extends to the entitlement to Black bodies, particularly to Black women's bodies.[8]

Case study: Julie

A study group is joined by one person of color, the only one. She is Black and initially welcomed by the group, which is keen to have someone of a "different" background. Julie, the newest group member, quickly notices microaggressions and other forms of exclusionary behavior that contradict verbalized discourses of **social inclusion** *the group holds dear. She raises the matter and attempts to get her peers to understand the impact of their behavior on her. Although she appears to be listened to, there is no verbal engagement with her experience. The covert behaviors remain, and raising the matter results in her being ignored and eventually marginalized. Julie becomes overtly distressed, angry, and emotionally uncontained and is eventually excluded from the group.*

Beverley Stobo, one of very few Black group analysts (specialists in group dynamics and processes), suggests that the silence that occurs when racism is called out serves to regulate and manage the anxiety it produces.[9] This silence holds a contentious space between white groups and Black people, according to Stobo. A space that holds the fear and terror of something that is too difficult, if not impossible, to name: shared trauma-laden histories of **imperialism**, colonialism, and enslavement. What is feared and too painful to put into words is a discovery or acknowledgment of racism.

We can use this formulation to understand Julie's experience and the group's responses to her. Julie was initially welcomed into the group, which no doubt saw itself as liberal and possibly above racism. Unsurprisingly, as Julie tried to articulate the racism, which was becoming apparent and targeted at her, these dynamics could not be contained. The group was conflicted about its racism and could neither express it directly nor confront it when invited to. As Julie attempted to make conscious the racism by directly confronting it, the difficulty in communication—the group disturbance—was located in her. She was selected to carry the burden of it alone. Containing the disturbance led to her becoming uncontained. She became distressed while white group members could, through their lack of emotional display, maintain a facade of objectivity, emotional maturity, detachment, and separation from the disturbance or problem they had co-created in the first place and which belonged to them. They succeeded in excluding Julie and therefore in splitting off from their racism.

SCAPEGOATS: THE CONSEQUENCE OF NAMING THE PROBLEM

British Australian feminist professor Sara Ahmed teaches us that when we speak of a problem, we become the problem.[10] In other words, speakers of problems become problems who speak. In every case of scapegoating, there is displacement and misdirection. Often uncomfortable or unacceptable feelings such as anger, envy, and shame are displaced and redirected onto another member, a colleague, often a peer but not always a more vulnerable person or group. The scapegoat can then be persecuted, bullied, or treated unfairly as those who project onto them are able to discharge their own (uncontained and unmetabolized) thoughts and feelings.[11]

Some of the conditions associated with scapegoating include

1. blame culture where there is a need to quickly find someone to blame when things go wrong or not according to plan
2. highly hierarchical cultures in which power is unequally distributed and decision-making is more vertical than horizontal
3. distressed contexts in which individuals may be experiencing high levels of stress and anxiety, perhaps because of organizational restructuring, change, or any increased sense of insecurity
4. contexts of underrepresentation in which some groups or individuals may be demographically isolated or "the only one"

INTERNALIZING PROJECTIONS

When we think about projections as a defense mechanism it is important to remember that they may or may not stick to the recipient. In psychology we call the process of making projections stick **projective identification**. With projective identification, the feelings, impulses, thoughts, or fantasies stick because they are forced onto the recipient to make them feel or behave in a way that is consistent with the projection.[12] For example, if someone projects Otherness onto me, and I identify with the projection, I will feel out of place. If someone projects inferiority onto me, and it sticks, I will feel inferior or inadequate. As a result, the recipient of the projection experiences an intrusion into their psychic space, a breach of their psychological boundaries.

We can use colonialism as a frame to make sense of the opening scenario. The group reaction to a Black body's entry into a white space triggered a visceral response and with it the suffocating sense of being excluded. Even in the absence of words, we can put the spotlight on dynamics that are often silenced. Firstly, there is that strong sense of déjà vu. We may relate it to colonial scripts or racist stereotypes such as the Black body as a trespasser or an oddity and therefore an object of scrutiny. Returning to a social psychology perspective on trauma and the group-level wounds that may be left on whole cultural or ethnic groups can help us make sense of our ongoing collective struggle in naming and containing racism and the anxiety that can arise from confronting white supremacy.[13]

TRAUMA AND THE BODY

There is no doubt that trauma has devastating consequences for our physical health and makes us more vulnerable to chronic illnesses. The psychological and physical responses to adverse experiences and trauma make us prone to long-term physical health problems. Those with a history of trauma are about three times more likely to experience conditions such as irritable bowel syndrome, chronic pain, and chronic fatigue syndrome.[14] Trauma, chronic stress, and racism have also been linked to several other health conditions, including cardio-vascular disease, obesity, diabetes, and cancer.[15]

The impact of chronic stress

Writing chapter 2, "Black Minds," I came to the realization that the Black scholars who most influenced me, and who dedicated their lives to combating the cancer that is racism, had died of cancer. Fanon died of leukemia in 1961. Feminist author Audre Lorde died of breast cancer in 1992. In 1987, author James Baldwin passed from stomach cancer. In 1998, civil rights activist Kwame Ture died of prostate cancer. I remember reading long ago about the autopsy following the assassination of Dr. Martin Luther King Jr. The autopsy revealed that although King was just thirty-nine when he was killed, he had the heart of a sixty-year-old. Even at the time, it was thought that the stress of fighting racism had taken its toll. White supremacy had worn out his heart. The symbolism of an illness or foreign body that invades us is a potent one. It mirrors the workings of anti-Blackness in society.

As far as cancer inequality goes, Black Americans have the highest death rate and shortest survival rate of any racial or ethnic group in the US for most cancers.[16] In the UK, prostate cancer, the most common cancer in men, is two to three times more likely in Black men than their white counterparts. The prostate cancer death rate for Black men is twice as high. Black men also develop prostate cancer younger.[17] Black women's survival rate for any cancer is among the lowest.

There are serious biological consequences to racism and discrimination. These include a damaged immune system, chronic **inflammation**, and premature cell aging.[18] These have been linked to health inequalities. "Cellular aging" refers to cells' reduced ability to divide and proliferate. Cellular aging occurs in all organisms with the passing of time, although environmental factors such as stress have been shown to cause cellular damage and gradually cause loss of cellular functions and eventually cell death.

Telomeres are DNA sequences that are found at both ends of a chromosome. Each time a cell replicates, its telomeres become shorter until it eventually dies. Telomere length is correlated with chronological age and cumulative wear and tear, which is generally due to stress. Several studies have found that, regardless of other health or socioeconomic backgrounds, experiences of racism are linked to shorter telomeres and that the more frequent the experiences, the faster the shortening of telomeres. In other words, experiences of discrimination accelerate biological wear and tear.[19]

Inflammation

Our body is designed to defend against pathogens—bacteria, viruses, and substances that appear foreign and harmful—via our immune system. A pathogen is a biological agent that causes disease or illness. When we are exposed to a new pathogen, we produce what is called an inflammatory immune response. Cortisol, a potent anti-inflammatory that helps us fight inflammation, is produced. However, when we're exposed to stressors or threats, we also produce cortisol and experience fear or perceived threat to safety, status, or well-being. The production of cortisol and other hormones in such situations is adaptive and promotes survival. It prepares our body for a fight-or-flight (or freeze) response.

However, chronic stress leads to hyper-physiological levels of cortisol, which is believed to reduce the effectiveness of cortisol to regulate both the inflammatory and immune responses. This is because it decreases tissue sensitivity to cortisol, leading to constant tissue breakdown and impairment of the immune system such as our immune response attacking our own cells, rendering those who experience chronic stress less able to fight off infections due to systemic inflammation and chronically elevated cortisol levels.

Racism (which is a chronic stressor) has been found to increase chronic inflammation among Black Americans. Although inflammation is nature's way to protect organisms from threats to their health, high levels of inflammation impair our ability to respond to threats from the outside. They can promote heart attacks, neurodegenerative diseases, and metastatic cancers. A study found that racism alone may account for 50 percent of the increased inflammation among Black

Americans. Reducing chronic stress decreases inflammation in the body and associated cortisol levels, which may reduce the risk not only of us developing chronic diseases but also of dying younger.[20] In the US alone, at the time of writing, over five hundred thousand people have died of COVID-19, with Black people disproportionately impacted. Research in the UK has shown that Black groups may be up to four times more likely to die of COVID-19 due to structural racism.[21] The physical impact of racism creates psychological trauma, which can be expected, in turn, to affect Black people's capacity to fight infections and to lead to further deaths, thus more trauma.

MISTRUST AND NEGLECT

In the US, medical mistrust has been found to be associated with delays in Black American men accessing routine health visits for blood pressure and cholesterol screenings.[22] Black men who report experiences of racism are much more likely to delay routine medical appointments overall. People who show more medical mistrust are much less likely to make use of preventative health interventions. The body-mind split is once more challenged.[23] Our communities know that the health inequalities that plague Black groups simply cannot be separated from racism. We also know that the body cannot thrive when the mind is under assault. Similarly, the mind cannot thrive when the body hurts. The health disparities that affect Black communities (such as the higher prevalence of chronic illnesses and disability or the higher mortality rates from most illnesses and diseases) clearly do not spare Black women. In addition, gendered and pregnancy-related injustice have been widely noted:

1. Black women are reported to be 3–4 times more likely to die from pregnancy-related complications than their white counterparts.
2. Black women are also 3–4 times more likely to suffer from a severe disability following childbirth when compared with white women.

3. Black women of childbearing age are twice more likely to suffer from infertility when compared to the general population in the US.

4. Black women are underrepresented in clinical trials that require consent and are overrepresented in studies that do not.

5. Black women are less likely to receive appropriate levels of painkillers than both white and Hispanic women despite reporting higher levels of pain after delivery.[24]

Also part of the picture: we see our doctors when our conditions are more advanced, often lethally so. These patterns have been found irrespective of healthcare access and health insurance, and they exist in the UK where the use of healthcare services is free at the point of access. In this state of affairs, a mixture of structural racism, distrust of health services, and intergenerational trauma is likely at play. Patterns of self-neglect are also a factor. If we have been harmed and abused, we are much more likely to relate to ourselves with contempt and violence and therefore to continue the cycle of abuse. There is ample evidence that suggests that trauma survivors are much more likely to self-harm, misuse substances, become reckless with their life and health, and basically behave in self-destructive ways. Often this is to manage difficult emotions, to self-medicate, or to cope with or distract oneself from the traumatic memories or experiences we can't escape from internally or externally. Self-harming behaviors can be a way of escaping pain. Sometimes too they are about rage-filled self-hate.

SUMMARY

1.

Racism hurts the Black body. Bessel van der Kolk argues that our body keeps the score and that it continues to tell stories that we cannot articulate. No understanding of racism and racial trauma can ever be complete without an examination of physical manifestations. We therefore need to pay attention to the Black body.

2.

The legacy of colonialism "entitles" white people to Black bodies. This can leave us vulnerable to boundary violations. Protecting our boundaries is important to protect ourselves from the harm of racism.

3.

Patterns of self-neglect need to be closely monitored. People who are poorly treated by society tend to treat themselves in similarly unkind ways. This may be interpreted as an internalization of racism or displacement of anger and rage toward ourselves.

4.

Bodily and psychological experiences help us understand racism. Racial violence is enacted through space, symbolically and nonverbally. The existence of an embodied racial (sub)consciousness and of racial bodily memory that are inseparable from our social and historical consciousness needs to be taken seriously.

5.

Trusting our body and treating it with kindness is an important step in reducing the harm of racial violence, particularly the more subtle bodily manifestations of racism.

....

In the next chapter, "Raising Black Children," we consider some of the challenges of parenting a child in the context of white supremacy and look more closely at the impact of racial trauma across generations.

RACE REFLECTIONS

The relationship between our environment and our body and the ways we may come to be physically harmed by racism are complex. This section gives you the opportunity to reflect and develop skills to help resist and protect your health and your body from racism.

What have you found most troubling in this chapter?

You may want to explore the bodily responses, images, and thoughts that came to you and explore what they might take you back to. Please use the Race Reflections reflective model (p. 183) to help you.

_____

_____

_____

_____

_____

To recover from trauma, it is important to connect and trust our body. Body-centered activities like deep-breathing exercises help us regulate our internal states and restore and repair the connection between our minds and our bodies.

How does your body respond to experiences of racism? For some of us, it is our heart or our stomach. For others, it is the head that holds the distress. Identifying where in our body we hold the racial distress can help us provide targeted relaxation. You could consider using an intentional soothing or healing touch for the areas you tend to tense while you practice some relaxation. Record your bodily response here.

_____

_____

_____

_____

_____

We have seen that treating our body harshly or neglecting our physical health can be a reproduction of societal contempt and can increase health inequality and the burden of disability and chronic health.

How do you tend to relate to your body? What tone of voice do you use? Think about the ways you might have been punishing, neglectful, and/or abusive toward your body and what may need to change for you to have a more supportive relationship with your body.

_____

_____

_____

_____

_____

We have seen that the Black body is vulnerable to becoming the repository of others' fantasies, fears, and disowned material.

What bodily experience did you have that you now feel may be accounted for by you taking in other people's "stuff"? Reflect on these experiences, and try to identify patterns. This will provide an opportunity for you to put psychological boundaries in place. Record your thoughts below.

_____

_____

_____

_____

_____

ACTION POINT

CELEBRATE YOUR BODY

Knowing what you know about the Black body may trigger mixed emotions and perhaps even a sense of grief for the ways in which you might have treated your body.

Your action point: Now that you have finished reading this chapter, start a new relationship with your body. You may find writing a letter to yourself helpful. As you write, you may find the following guidelines useful. Imagine that you are someone who loves everything about you deeply and unconditionally:

1. What might they say about your body?

2. What soothing words might they use to describe the part of yourself you dislike?

3. How might they encourage you to do better when it comes to how you have learned to treat yourself?

4. What might they be proud of in relation to your body?

Once you build a picture of this person, try every day to be more like them until the distinction between you two disappears.

CHAPTER 5

RAISING BLACK CHILDREN

When she was six, my daughter came home upset and asked me to redo her hair. She had gone to school with two ponytails, two Afro puffs to be precise, and two cornrows at the front and two at the back of her head. She looked alarmed and anxious. "The teacher said my hair is too big—I can't wear a hat, and I need to change it, or I won't be in the school play," she exclaimed. I reassured her. I said I would not change her hairstyle and that her hair was perfectly fine. The following day her father took her to school and explained to the teacher her comments were out of line and that she needed to be included in the school play whether her hair could fit into a hat or not. Furthermore, he showed her how to gather her Afro puffs into one to fit a hat. In the afternoon I picked her up, and one of her braids at the back of her head had been cut. She had not realized. Only the teacher had touched her hair, to put it in a hat. I contacted the school; they had no idea. The head teacher wanted to double-check that her braid had indeed been cut, in case I was mistaken, I presume. She agreed, then confirmed that children had had no access to scissors. I explained to her the conflict around my daughter's Afro hair. I insinuated that this might have been an act of malicious retaliation. The head teacher was outraged. She could not fathom that racism could be taking place in her school. This was beyond the realm of possibility. She disclosed to me that she had mixed-race grandchildren and since she herself as head teacher had grandchildren of color whom she loved very much, no racism could possibly be taking place in her school. We never found out who had cut my girl's hair. We never heard anything further either. This chapter tackles the challenges of raising Black children amid racism and racial trauma.

RAISING BLACK CHILDREN

We often say there is no manual that can really teach you how to be a parent. That is certainly true. The aim of this chapter is not to provide a manual for parents on how to raise Black children. To a large extent, the task of raising Black children is the task of raising any children. We do the best we can with what we have and what we know. Nonetheless, in addition to general concerns around supporting Black children to become independent adults, the task of the Black parent is also to help their children navigate racism and, as far as is possible, to protect them from its harm. No blueprint to facilitate this overly complex task can ever exist. Black children are usually invisible from conversations around racism's traumatic effects. Few studies look at the impact of racism across a lifespan. This chapter aims to center the needs of Black children.

Black children start to become aware of race and racism at an incredibly young age. Our racialization or socialization to racial constructions as social beings starts early. By the age of three or four, often much sooner, children become aware of skin color. They start to understand racial categories and show evidence of racial biases and preferences consistent with general societal attitudes. They begin to identify with one or several racial groups. By age four most are adept at recognizing racial differences and what they signify for them. These may include awareness of the differential treatment they are afforded by people around them because of the color of their skin. Children's racial socialization is influenced by their parents' own experience of racism, racial attitudes, and their coping or survival strategies.[1] Hence our child-rearing practices, identity, history, and social positioning are, to a large extent, inseparable.

SCHOOL VIOLENCE

There is nothing more heartbreaking to a parent than leaving your child at a gate of a school knowing they will be subjected to racism and fearing that if you challenge the school, your child may be subjected to even more racism. Witnessing their children experience racism can lead parents to racial trauma and/or activate memories of their own experience of racist violence in school or in other settings. Which then also has the potential to lead to further distress in children, leading to a cycle of wounding. That introductory extract at the start of the chapter is from an article I wrote in June 2019, "On School, Institutional Racism and Everyday Violence." The article came about after I was heavily trolled on social media for suggesting that schools are as structurally and institutionally racist as the police and that they are continuing, by and large, to get away with it. Teachers reacted defensively to my tweets to assert that they had never seen or experienced racism throughout their career. I wrote this piece to challenge their narrative but also to force many of those who refused to confront the realities of so many Black parents to see it. It is interesting that after the piece was published, most, if not all, of those who were initially engaged in denial turned silent. Hundreds of messages followed, mainly from Black parents and other parents of color. Many shared their stories of racism in school.

It is concerning to me that even though what Black families experience is quite common, white people and schools continue to act shocked when we speak out.[2] The racial disparity in the US education system is widespread and well-documented. Several factors lead to inequality in education access, experience, and outcomes. They include government policies, informal segregation, unequal resource allocation to schools along racial lines, and teachers' bias and racism.

Recent data from the Department of Education's Civil Rights Database suggests a significant rise in racial disparities in Black students' arrests and referrals to police.

- During the 2016–17 school year, schools suspended 2.7 million students. This number was about 100,000 students lower than when federal data was last collected, in 2013–14.
- Black boys made up 25 percent of all students suspended from school, and Black girls made up another 14 percent—even

though each group only accounted for about 8 percent of all students.

- Black children, about 15 percent of all students during 2015–16, were 31 percent of those arrested or referred to police for in-school behavior.[3]
- Data from 2013–14 collected by the US Department of Education's Office of Civil Rights shows that Black K–12 students are 3.8 times more likely than their white peers to receive one or more out-of-school suspensions.[4]
- Three factors have been found to increase risks of preschool exclusions: being Black, being male, and looking older than their classmates (*Foundation for Child Development*, 2005).
- Teachers have been found to be more likely to **stereotype** Black students as troublemakers and recommend harsher discipline than white counterparts engaging in similar infractions after repeated misbehavior (*Psychological Science*, 2015).
- In 2014, the high school graduation rate for white students was 87 percent and 73 percent for Black students, according to the National Center for Education Statistics.
- Teachers have been found to be less likely to spot Black students who excel academically (*Journal of Public Administration Research and Theory*, 2016).
- When evaluating the same Black student, white teachers are 12 percent less likely to predict that the student will finish high school, and 30 percent less likely to predict the student will graduate from college, than Black teachers (*Economics of Education Review*, 2016).

The above inequalities are the tip of the iceberg.[5] Schools are arguably a pillar of white supremacy and a site of trauma. This is what the expression "school-to-prison pipeline" seeks to highlight, that school policies and practices create conditions that increase the likelihood of social exclusion and later incarceration, to protect the dominance, superiority, and privileges of white groups.[6] So, what does it say to us as

Black parents that when we reflect on racism, so many white teachers still feel the need to defend, argue, and deny?

Influenced by Kwame Ture, the late English judge William Macpherson defined institutional racism as "the collective failure of an organization to provide an appropriate and professional service to people because of their color, culture or ethnic origin." He further added that it can be seen in "processes, attitudes and behaviour which amount to discrimination through unwitting prejudice, ignorance, thoughtlessness and racist stereotyping which disadvantages minority ethnic people."[7]

ABSENT DADS, BOSSY MOMS

There are enduring stereotypes about Black parenthood. The absent father is such a trope. And while this idea is heavily peddled in popular culture and political discourses both in the UK and the US, many have challenged this narrative with facts. For example, Josh Levs's "No, Most Black Kids Are Not Fatherless" challenged the myth using data from the US Centers for Disease Control and Prevention. Levs showed that most Black fathers do in fact live with their children (2.5 million versus 1.7 million who don't).[8] And that, regardless of living arrangements, Black fathers are among the most involved in the life of their children. So, where does this trope come from?

In 1965, a report by sociologist Daniel Patrick Moynihan, titled *The Negro Family: The Case for National Action*, was published. The report framed Black parents as the principal cause of an alleged culture of pathology in Black American families. There was no attempt at identifying structural racism or other barriers that made mothering while Black challenging or at addressing the structural racism plaguing Black communities, even though the report predates the end of the civil rights movement. It is argued that this work contributed to society seeing Black American mothers as deficient, lacking, and pathological.[9]

In the UK, too, researchers have found similar stereotypes to be pervasive.[10] Following the fatal stabbing of a fourteen-year-old in 2012 as he stepped off a bus in London, Black British MP David Lammy made a controversial speech calling for a more active form of father-hood in the Black community.[11] He argued that focusing on fathers was the key to tackling knife crimes in the capital. That it could help reduce educational "under-achievement," disproportionate exclusion rates, and high crime rates among Black youth. The major issue with Lammy's speech was that it was decontextualized and thus presented stereotypical narratives that have the power to do much more harm than good. It is correct, in the context of the UK, that Black children are more likely to live in unmarried households. However, nontradi-tional households do not necessarily translate to absent fathers nor do absent fathers translate to criminality. Such questionable conclusions paint Black fathers as irresponsible, immoral, and unbothered about their children's welfare. Instead, in one of the largest reviews of youth knife crime, researchers found that adverse childhood experiences, poor mental health, discrimination, and inequality are the main factors associated with youth violence.[12]

TALKING TO BLACK CHILDREN ABOUT RACISM

Racism is not the only challenge Black parents face, but it is one that cannot simply be ignored. Parents can be at a loss about how best to support their children when it comes to racist experiences. Should they have "**The Talk**," or should they not, and, if so, how? For way too many, it seems, this dilemma is resolved by not talking about racism at all. Or by delaying the conversation for as long as possi-ble, often until the child is in their teens. Or even not until the child reaches adulthood. Sometimes these conversations never happen. And although we can easily rationalize the upholding of silences, they re-sult in Black children being left to manage the anxiety and distress that anti-Blackness creates without any guidance or support. They are therefore left vulnerable to racial trauma. The Talk is mainly an Amer-ican cultural practice, born out of centuries of racial oppression on American soil. It is not clear how widespread the practice is outside the US, but it appears to be less common abroad.

To test that, I conducted a study with Black people before writing this chapter and asked research participants whether they had had a conversation about racism as children, and, if so, what age they were when it occurred. Over seven hundred people engaged in the survey, and it generated several conversations online. The broad trends of the survey were as follows:

- **AGE:** While more people reported being spoken to about racism (about 60 percent), about 40 percent said they did not have this conversation or that they did not remember having it. About 40 percent of those who had the conversation were nine to twelve years old.
- **ETHNICITY:** Differences across various Black groups came to light. Generally, Black people in the UK seem much less likely to talk to their children about racism than Black people in the US, and Black African groups in the UK are much less likely to report having these conversations than those in the Black Caribbean.
- **IMPLICATIONS:** Not discussing racism seriously disadvantages Black children. It affects awareness of and preparation for managing racist encounters, and it deprives them of support. As we will cover later, this denial has been linked to mental health challenges later in life.

ADVERSE CHILDHOOD EXPERIENCES

Trauma can happen at any age. Being told by a friend they are not allowed to play with us because we are Black. A teacher wrongly accusing us of cheating because we produced a piece of work deemed above our intellectual abilities. Being marked down or disciplined for completely arbitrary and subjective reasons, often because a teacher cannot fathom a gifted Black child, particularly when they are non-deferential and irreverent. Being discouraged from going to university. Being repeatedly punished more harshly at schools for similar infractions committed by white pupils. Additional common experiences include witnessing

Black men being disproportionately stopped and searched by the police, hearing parents being racially abused, and seeing loved ones being discriminated against. All this creates a context of chronic stress that can cumulatively have a traumatic effect on Black children and create a climate of **adverse childhood experiences (ACEs)**.[13] "ACE" is the term used to describe distressing experiences that happen to us before we are eighteen and have lifelong negative emotional and physical effects. ACEs are attracting increased scrutiny in public health because they have been found to be linked to health inequality between racial groups. For many parents, then, talking about racism to younger children can be a challenge.

This is something I experienced firsthand. After my mother and sister were horribly assaulted, after the screams, after the distress and terror, a deafening silence engulfed us all. We did not speak about the horror we had all witnessed. We spoke, of course, but we did not talk as a family about racism. We did not talk about it as a community. Even at school, where everyone would have evidently heard about it, since so many children were present, silence reigned. My mother's face remained deformed for months. I can still see the white of one of her eyes tainted with blood. The family, the school, and our community proceeded to behave as though nothing had happened. No one, it seemed, could put words to the assault. We were all left to process this painful event together but alone and in silence. The perpetrator was jailed, and my mother's face and head slowly recovered. She regained her beauty. It was only several years after this incident that my mother broached the subject of racism with us. I think by then I was nine or ten. It was decades after these initial conversations that as a family we broke the silence on the assaults. Over thirty years had passed. We had all remembered and forgotten different bits. This is what trauma does. It shatters memories and makes it difficult to put the pieces together. Nonetheless, as we made space for it, a collective memory started to emerge from the silence.[14] As we have seen, silence is often a sign of trauma, of our capacity to make sense of being overwhelmed by horror or fear.[15] Or a sign that we would rather not speak into existence our experience, wish it had not taken place. The ubiquity of silence following traumatic experiences became obvious in my work with various survivor groups, including survivors of sexual or gender-related violence, survivors of war and persecution, and survivors of other overwhelming experiences. This is a phenomenon that is well-documented.[16] So much so that it is often said that silence is the voice of trauma.

Case study: The school that tried to end racism

In June 2020, in the UK, Channel 4 launched a documentary series that followed year seven pupils at a school in South London, Glenthorne High School, for three weeks.[17] The school ran an experiment aiming to tackle racial bias and racism. As part of the program, conversations on race were encouraged in segregated groups, and children were followed home to observe them share with their parents their reflections on the program. In one episode, Bright, a young Black boy, returns home and discusses his experience of racism with his mother. He fidgets and looks ill at ease, rarely making eye contact with her. At times he seems to stutter. We see him on the verge of tears as he tries to find the words to communicate to his mother his experience of being repeatedly stopped and searched and racially profiled by the police, despite his young age.

Bright seems to be in his early to mid-teens. He is obviously smart and understands he is the victim of racism. He is confident outside of this exchange. As he speaks, his mother watches him, also looking somewhat ill at ease as he says: "Whenever you go into a shop you feel like, 'Oh, hopefully I don't get stopped today,' and it just gets to you." She is initially silent but appears to be listening intently. Then her response to Bright leaves the audience feeling something is disjointed. She exclaims, "This is based on what has happened before; the shopkeeper is not lying, and you should not be angry." In her attempt to comfort Bright, the mother rationalizes the racism and invalidates Bright's experience. Bright becomes more agitated as he continues to struggle to be heard.

PARENT-CHILD CONFLICTS

This scene is gut-wrenching. Many found it upsetting and took to social media to voice their distress both at Bright's regular experience of racism and at his mother's response. Others were quick to criticize her and connected to Bright's struggle to be understood. My heart broke for Bright, but I also felt compassion toward his mother. Based on her accent, my impression is that she is a West African migrant. She is a mother who was attempting to manage the racist experiences her child brings home, while probably being unprepared. A mother who appears disconnected from her son's lived reality. A mother who inadvertently silences to soothe.

The story of Bright and his mother in the UK is reminiscent of the story of sixteen-year-old Michael Singleton and his mother in the US. On April 29, 2015, Michael had left after Freddie Gray's funeral to protest with his friends and an estimated seventy-five to one hundred school-age children, against the instructions of the mother, who wanted him home straight after school. In a video that went viral, Toya Graham, Michael's mother, is seen meeting her son on the streets and smacking him and screaming at him for disobeying her. The clip of Graham berating and hitting Michael led to Graham being widely acclaimed in the US media for disciplining her son. Yet something is amiss. That something becomes clearer in the interview the pair gave to ABC News. To explain her action, Graham says to her son, "As long as I have breath in my body, you will not be on the streets selling drugs." Then she says, "You're just not going live like that. Not with me."[18]

These words and sentiments have echoes of that earlier parent-child disconnect in the Channel 4 program. Here too it is clear that the mother wants what is best for her son, to protect him from violence and criminality and instill in him a respect for order. Still, something is not quite adding up. Michael's motivation and the lived experience of growing Black and male and recurrently confronting police injustice is not engaged with. At least not in the interview. The fear Graham verbalizes, it appears, is disconnected from Michael's lived reality.

So, Bright's mother is not alone in struggling, and neither is he. They are both struggling, but their struggle is separate. In the UK, and from what I have found through both my research and clinical work on racial trauma, that very same separate struggle is often featured. For most people I come across, there is little evidence of having had The Talk, contrary to what appears in the US.

Where immigration is concerned, important differences can exist in terms of worldview between parents and their children simply due to age, generation, and diaspora. The Black British population is primarily composed of descendants of immigrants from the Caribbean and Africa who in the main migrated to the UK after the Second World War. Today, according to the last Office for National Statistics census, Black residents in the UK make up about 3 percent of the country's population, and 13 percent of those are born abroad.[19] In the UK, 95 percent of Black Africans arrived after 1981, whereas for Black Caribbean groups the percentage was 61 percent. The fact that Black Caribbean families have been coping with white supremacy in Britain for longer than Black Africans may translate into them being better able to articulate British racism.

These patterns of migration matter a great deal in the context of Blackness in Britain. They are often amplified by broader histories of displacement, alienation, and colonial violence. For a significant large number of Black families, one or both parents were not born in Britain or Europe. Perhaps they emigrated from the Caribbean or from Africa. And while there is absolutely no doubt that white supremacy is a global phenomenon operational at a geopolitical level, meaning that it exists across nations and is deeply ingrained in the fabric of former colonies, parents' racial politics and experiences of racism may be very different from those of their children. These differences may lead to the kind of conflicting exchanges we witnessed in "the school that tried to end racism" case study.

Stories of migration and experiences of racism are vastly different across the diaspora. They depend on the host countries, how recent the migration is, and, of course, the historical context. We do know that migration and displacement cause multiple challenges for Black family units alongside the usual difficulties of raising children. Not least: mental health. Migrant groups' vulnerability to psychological distress is well documented by decades of research.[20] There are many factors that account for that vulnerability: The loss of familiarity and social networks. Racialized xenophobia. In the UK, the Windrush scandal comes to mind. Black people are a growing segment of the immigrant population in the United States. Although discourses around migration in the US are centered around people from South and Central America, the number of Black migrants to the US is rising sharply. There were 816,000 Black immigrants in 1980, 2.4 million in 2010, and 4.2 million in 2016. Currently, it is estimated that about 10 percent of the Black population in the United States was born outside of the country.

Undocumented Black migrants are also more likely to be over-policed, incarcerated, or deported.[21] In the UK, 76 percent of Black immigrants are deported on criminal grounds, compared to 45 percent of all immigrants. This is the result of hostility, the stigma and marginalization encountered in the country. Social deprivation and/or economic challenges can also lead to or exacerbate racial trauma. This trauma often echoes traumatic violence experienced in the country of origin, particularly for forced migrants and refugees. Sometimes parents who are migrants and have left persecutory contexts may not be prepared to listen to criticisms related to the new country because of a need to idealize their new home in order to feel safe and justify the major life changes immigration has brought. They may simply not have the emotional capacity to cope with additional trauma.

Generational differences have a deep impact. Research suggests, for example, that those comprising the so-called second generation of migrants are much more aware of the reality of racial injustice. They aspire less to assimilate and are more vocal about their entitlement to justice and equal treatment. This makes sense if we consider that older generations may not necessarily consider Britain or the "host country" as their new home but instead as a temporary place of abode. A place primarily to work with a view to returning "back home" to retire. Similarly, parents may feel that the struggles of everyday racism experienced by their offspring do not compare with their own struggles, especially in cases where parents have experienced persecution, torture, extreme poverty, or colonial racism. They may inadvertently minimize their children's difficulties. A communication gap may start to emerge that can have profound implications for the quality of parent-child relationships. It can alienate children and foster further silence. For all these reasons, migrants' families often experience relational difficulties.[22] Clearly, as we have seen with the story of Michael, parent-child conflicts can and do occur outside of migration configurations too.

ATTACHMENT AND HISTORICAL BONDS

In chapter 2, we touched on Post Traumatic Slave Syndrome and the survival scripts that descendants of enslaved people have inherited from their forebears. Such patterns have also shaped parenting and family functioning within Black America.

One of slavery's enduring legacies is family malfunction imposed by the system. Attachment and bonds were severely disrupted as fathers were frequently sold away or unable to care for their offspring or family, and mothers were rarely left adequate time to bond and form healthy attachments with their infants and young children. Further, fears and normalized sadistic abuses plagued parenting experiences. Scholars have argued that intergenerational wounds can still be observed in the ongoing challenges the Black family structure may experience. These wounds are visible in the widespread insecure attachments between parents and children, in the dominance of fear and/or shame in the raising of children, and at times in the normalizing of punishing and abusive child-rearing practices such as the widespread acceptance of child "whupping."

Cleary, slavery and enslavement have also left enduring marks on **attachment**. Attachment is the bond between a child and their caregivers, particularly the mother. It was British psychologist and psychoanalyst John Bowlby who initiated clinical interest in attachment.[23] He described attachment as a "lasting psychological connectedness between human beings." This connectedness is an evolutionary mechanism to ensure the survival of the species that he suggested had a huge impact on the child's mental health, lasting well into adulthood.

American Canadian psychologist Mary Ainsworth examined children's responses to being (artificially) separated from their caregivers in a laboratory setting for the purpose of the experiment.[24] The levels of anxiety and distress they displayed, as well as their responses when reuniting with the caregiver, were found to be a reliable source of information to assess the nature of the bond that exists between them. A "secure" attachment helps the child to begin to develop abstract or symbolic "mastery." In time, as the infant internalizes the soothing attention and care they receive when in need, they learn to tolerate distress without undue dread. This helps them to later feel safe and trusting in intimate relationships. There is a great deal of research on attachment in the field of psychology, most of which is premised on the idea that the first relationship, usually with our mother, shapes our internal configurations and becomes an enduring relational template that we use to manage relationships and know what to expect in the world.

The attachment bond is shaped by the way the infant responded to early relational experiences. An infant whose distress is contained, and whose needs are cared for, learns to trust both their internal world and the world around them. Feeling contained, nurtured, and safe is essential for optimal cognitive development. Feeling secure helps us think.

A few fundamental characteristics of slavery bear direct relevance when considering attachment, particularly for those who are direct descendants of enslaved Africans. For centuries, on the African continent, millions saw loved ones kidnapped or sold away overnight.[25] Once in the Americas, being enslaved meant living under the constant threat of separation. Children could be sold away at a moment's notice. Enslaved women were rarely afforded time to bond with their infants since they were expected shortly after giving birth to return to the fields. Dissociating from the pain of separation was necessary to survive.

Attachment challenges are amplified by immigration. The ease with which Black African and Black Caribbean parents can leave children behind via immigration, the dissociation from the distress this causes, not only speaks of punishing economic realities and geopolitical inequalities but also says something about the normalization of disrupted attachment, of separation, and the numbing of distress. The collective violence our ancestors were subjected to. The survival strategies they perfected to keep alive have not completely disappeared, far from it, and they continue to affect family dynamics, such as causing conflicts, resentment, or envy between siblings when some were left behind "back home" and others were born in or brought to the West. Although we can sometimes fool ourselves into believing that these times are far behind us today, in the history of modern civilization Black groups have spent more time enslaved and colonized than they have spent time free.

INTERNALIZED RACISM

We usually speak of internalized racism to refer to the way people of color accept the veracity of the white supremacy as ideology and inevitably the notion of their inherent inferiority.[26] It is when we take actions that reproduce the system of racism. We can see internalized racism in our preference for lighter-skinned individuals and the hierarchy we uphold around skin shade so that many of us hold in higher regard those with proximity to whiteness. We can see internalized racism in our veneration of white European cultures, values, and worldviews. We can see internalized racism in our drive to assimilate and aim to resemble or sit next to the master. Some see internalized racism as one of the most common, yet least studied, features of racism. The subject is fraught with taboo, shame, and avoidance, leading to many misconceptions and unmet psychological needs. Most Black people have learned that we need to be twice as good as our white counterparts to be deemed good enough to stand underneath them. Similarly, it is not unusual for Black parents to mirror (consciously or otherwise) the harsh treatment society metes out to Black boys. To respond with a punishing rhetoric to any lapse in conduct, particularly those associated with racial prejudices, out of fear that negative societal expectations and the dreaded stereotypes may materialize. This "double bind" can be used to make sense of internalized racism, the illusionary and implicit promise by white structures that Black people can escape the consequences of their Otherness by disowning their "difference." Their Blackness.

Clearly internalized racism cannot be separated from issues of intergenerational trauma and issues of identification with the aggressor. A kind of Stockholm syndrome, some may say, can take place, where we feel compelled to identify with, relate to, and emulate those who harm to gain power and control. We may, therefore, link this double bind to **double consciousness**, seeing ourselves through our eyes but also through the eyes of white people.[27] All communities internalize the dominant beliefs of society, and therefore the expression "double consciousness" as exclusively applied to people of color is misleading. However, if staying silent means racism is not confronted and the status quo is maintained, then staying silent when harmed by racism is also a manifestation of internalized racism. But achieving the promise of the double bind is impossible. Audre Lorde believed that silence does not protect us. It cannot protect us because racism remains the operative system whether we name it or not. Its damage continues.

PARENTAL TRAUMA

It is difficult to put into words how difficult it is for many of us to deal with schools. I have repeatedly said that handling race-based conflicts in schools is one of the most difficult experiences to navigate as a Black mother. There is undoubtedly a triggering effect. When we have experienced racism at schools ourselves, seeing our children also experience it can be extremely distressing. So, of course, the temptation is to avoid facing things that remind us of our own experience or trauma. Furthermore, the availability and quality of support children are provided with will also be affected by their parents' experiences of racism at the time.

Chronic or severe stress, as we have seen, can have far-reaching consequences on the body, but it also affects family functioning.[28] It can affect closeness, patience, and availability. In some cases, chronic stress in parents can even lead to abuse and neglect. The chronicity of racism poses serious challenges to Black family units. It means that often as the child faces racism at school one or both of their parents may also be struggling with racism at work or at university, for example. If so, their emotional responsiveness to the child may well be compromised. When we are preoccupied with any racial injustices happening to us and we face chronic discrimination ourselves, our capacity to be there for our children can suffer.[29] In turn, children may learn that they should not "burden" an emotionally stretched parent. They will pick up cues on how the parent responds or speaks. We may well be unconsciously telling children we do not have capacity to hear.

PROTECTING BLACK CHILDREN

Black parents sometimes maintain silences or dismiss racism, consciously seeking to protect their children. Similarly, in my own research, participants often believed their parents were attempting to protect them. Protect their innocence, protect them from having distressing conversations, but, of course, that is not the whole story. Many may be convinced that speaking about racism will damage their children. That it will make children less able to function within white supremacy or cause them to lose ambition or confidence in themselves. I believe this was the case in my home when I was growing up. My parents believed that we were too young to understand, too young to face and deal with the terror of whiteness. They also placed high value on education. They would have done anything to protect our aspirations. Their silence, I am certain, was also born out of the desire not to discourage us. They wanted so badly to protect our life chances.

But the reality is that we were never fully protected. It was never within their gifts to protect us from white supremacy. Black parents do not have that power. We saw the differing treatment, the attitudes toward our parents. We heard their stories when they got home after work exhausted and complained about mundane acts of injustice and discrimination. And of course, we experienced racism directly too. Silence may be employed to protect parents from having to connect to feelings of powerlessness when it comes to the ability to safeguard their children from racism. It protects them from the hopelessness in seeing one's child experience the same traumas they or their ancestors did. This possibly explains in some the wish to delay for as long as possible the need to face it all. Children also often keep silent about their racist experiences, sometimes out of shame, often wanting to protect their parents by sparing them additional hurt and pain.

LANGUAGE AND SELF-CARE

One of the main reasons Black children need language and strategies to manage experiences of racism is because they are at risk of internalizing negative stereotypes. Thus, they are deprived of the opportunity to forge a sense of who they are, beyond what society and those around them may think and project onto them. All children are vulnerable to believing that they deserve or are responsible for mistreatment and violence that is done to them. Black children are no different. Silence fosters self-hate and breeds shame. A major task in supporting children and equipping them with what they need to build a positive racial identity, therefore, is giving them strategies to externalize what is put onto them in a racist society.

When Black children are not given tools to deal with negative messages they receive from others, their ideas of who they are will be constructed of combinations of environmental and societal discourses. These include stereotypes and negative expectations acquired from school and the media. Black children receive both covert and overt messages that tell them that they are intellectually deficient, frequently from teachers' biases.[30]

We cannot expect optimal cognitive development while we fail to support Black children with their experience of racism. The consequence of racism is often **anxiety**. Anxiety impairs our ability to learn, to concentrate and retain information. Silence and the denial of racism by parents have been shown to amplify anxiety.[31] When a child experiences a trauma in a context in which they have been taught they cannot trust or rely on their parents or carer for support, the world can suddenly seem very scary. Dangers and fears are often exaggerated as children attempt to fill blanks regarding what they do not understand or know. In silence, the child gets the message that there is something dreadful, unspeakable, and beyond the ability of the parent to help them with. In time they might learn that support cannot come from their loved ones. So not only is racism something we do not talk about; it is something we struggle with alone. Something seen as not being worth seeking support for. By extension, the message is that they will face incomprehensible experiences and that no one will be here to help. These expectations and relational patterns can be taken into adulthood and affect intimacy, security, and safety in relationships and in the world more generally. Finally, keeping silent about harm is not processing it. What is not processed is not healed. Many psychologists say that what a generation cannot bear tends to be passed on to burden the next generation. So, silence may well support the transmission of intergenerational trauma, continuing the circle of harm. The fact is that our fears are often amplified by the silence that surrounds us. Naming them and facing our discomfort can help us make space for these conversations.

SUMMARY

1.

Silence is all too often the response, the main survival or coping strategy after trauma. The complexities of supporting Black children, especially while parents themselves may be struggling with experiences of racism or with their own unprocessed trauma, need much attention.

2.

Silence is reproduced by society. In the psychology and mental health scholarship, the literature is thin. Parents and children are therefore left unsupported, a symptom itself of systemic racism. In that system, those who speak out and challenge racism can face punishment, discredit, and/or violence.

3.

If silence is forcefully enforced by society and has a long history, it is not something we can hold Black parents solely responsible for. Yet, as Black parents, we can do better. There is so much we cannot bear to face. There is so much we would rather not hear, too, partly because it takes us to our own painful histories.

4.

Racism will not be the only challenge Black families will need to negotiate. Of course, social deprivation is another factor for many, as is the intersection of migration-related challenges. This will greatly increase the level of stress a family is exposed to and impact their emotional availability and attachment. Silence is simply not an option.

....

In the next chapter, "Working While Black," we look at what it is like to navigate white workplaces as a Black employee, some of the ways racism manifests at work, and what we can do to support ourselves.

RACE REFLECTIONS

We saw that racism causes many challenges to the family unit and can affect our relationships with children. We need to tackle these challenges head-on to safeguard Black children's welfare. This section gives you the opportunity to reflect and develop skills to help resist and protect Black children from racism.

What have you found most troubling in this chapter?
You may want to explore your embodied responses and images and thoughts that came to you and explore what they might take you back to. Please use the Race Reflections reflective model (p. 183) to help you.

What have been your parents' and grandparents' formative experiences of racism? What stories of theirs have stayed with you?
What do you think they might have passed on to you about the world, and how do you relate to your fears? What has been helpful, and what has been less helpful? What might you want to pass on to younger generations, and what would you rather leave behind?

**What are your key fears when it comes to racism,
and how do they manifest?**

---

*It is important that you connect with potential fears and name them so
they do not leak into your relationship with your child/children. Our fears
can manifest in many ways, such as in overprotection or under-protection,
in harshness or invalidation. Please be curious about how your fears
may manifest.*

_____

_____

_____

_____

_____

**When it comes to conversations about racism with children,
what could you do better?**

---

*Reflect on the conversations you have had with younger Black people. What
could you do differently to be more supportive and validating? If you have
not had these conversations, consider what you might need to feel more
comfortable having them.*

_____

_____

_____

_____

_____

TALKING TO BLACK
CHILDREN ABOUT RACISM

A couple of things before you start . . .

Prepare emotionally

This may be both the simplest and the most difficult thing to do. It can be extremely difficult to confront racism as a parent. It may take us back to our own experience of racism and oppression. It may make some of us feel that we have somehow failed as a parent. Feelings of helplessness, power-lessness, and/or guilt about not having been able to shelter the child from the reality of oppression may arise. Some parents may even feel angry the child is responding in a way that they may see as unhelpful.

A range of feelings and emotions may be evoked, which will be picked up by the child. A lack of preparation could lead us to invalidate the child's experi-ence, or it could derail the conversation, distract, make us change the subject, or try to laugh things off.

Please resist. Silencing the child may assign shame to their experience and/ or teach them that the subject is taboo or could cause offense, embarrassment, or hurt to you. Consequently, the child may not bring the subject up again and may learn instead to keep this potentially troubling experience to themselves. Silencing the child might even reinforce any potential association between themselves, Blackness, and being "bad."

Engage on the child's level

Try to remain curious and open so you can meet the child where the child is at. Probe with open and neutral questions so that you can start to build a picture of the child's experience and belief system, such as the qualities that have been attributed to Blackness and whiteness. Ask your child how they make sense of experiences they may bring to you. But also be on the lookout for beliefs around responsibility and feelings of shame. If you start where your child is at, you will be better able to challenge problematic beliefs in due course and to provide relevant counter-narratives.

Part of engaging the child where they are at is remembering the child's age. Having a conversation with a five- or six-year-old is different from having a conversation with a fourteen-year-old. There is no need to expose younger children to violent, brutal, or graphic images or conversations that will likely in-crease their anxiety. But downplaying what teenagers are exposed to on social media or at school will not help build trust or meet the child's need.

Remember: balance matters

We can easily become preoccupied with racism, particularly when we are on the receiving end of it.

While this is understandable, it may lead us to overdo it when it comes to talking about racism. Please bear that in mind. It is also important that we remember that our behavior will have much more of an impact than our words. The way we respond to racism will teach children how to respond to racism. Similarly, how we treat children will teach them about how to expect to be treated in the world. There is a balance to be struck: by overfocusing on racism, on abuse, and on trauma-loaded conversations, we may do more harm than good.

So, it is important to help children connect with joy and beauty too. Being loved, nurtured, and attended to are probably the strongest buffers against racial trauma and help internalize safety. It is important to teach Black children that they are loved and that they are lovable and that they matter. This is arguably the most important message in fostering self-love.

10 TOP TIPS

1. **Start with thanking the child for their openness and courage.** This is important to reinforce the idea that your child was right to come to you and that you will be there whenever they experience racism and other difficult or confusing situations.
2. **Learn about child development in relation to challenging conversations on racism.** Some may find therapeutic support helpful, while others may be satisfied with doing their own research.
3. **Take the initiative.** Do not wait for the child to be "old enough" to start thinking about such conversations. It is also not helpful to wait for them to bring up racism. Your child may well be waiting for you to signal that it is okay to start the conversation, or they may want to protect you!
4. **Give yourself permission to grieve.** The most important part of preparing for conversations on racism is to allow yourself to grieve and be upset by the reality that you will likely have to help your child navigate anti-Blackness.
5. **Be reflective.** A central part of preparation is to be reflective around our own fears and our own experiences, to try not to project them onto the child. Carry out some of the exercises in this chapter and in chapter 1.
6. **Seek support—beforehand and afterwards.** It is completely understandable to feel uncertain and worried. Some preparation will stop you from feeling completely out of your depth. Who else can you discuss these experiences with? Is there another parent or family member who could offer reassurance and help you find the right words? Remember to look after your well-being too if your child is the victim of racism.
7. **Create a Black-centric home.** It is crucially important that Black children have access to positive role models who look like them. This environment signals to children that Blackness matters and that Blackness is beautiful. This will also help with the development of a more secure cultural identity and a healthy self-esteem. Further, art, books, and other cultural

products provide opportunities for parents to start to talk about history and racism in their own terms as opposed to being thrown in at the deep end because of a racist incident at school, for example.

8. **Show unconditional love to your child before, during, and after the conversation.** It is easy for parents to assume that their children know they are loved. But research suggests many adults never felt loved as children. It is absolutely vital that the context within which the conversations on racism take place is one in which the child feels loved because this will challenge racist messages and the hostile or hateful language or incidents you may need to discuss. Attentiveness, availability, kindness, compassion, and tone are often what children use to assess love.

9. **Create safety.** As much as it is within your power, ensure that your home and your relationship are safe when you are preparing to have a conversation about racism. Can you have it in a place and room where your child feels safe? Can you support your child with feeling as safe as possible after the conversation? Black children can benefit from basic relaxation and self-soothing skills.

10. **Do not sweat it! Trust yourself as a parent.** If you are attentive, seek to build your capacity, and develop like most parents do, you are likely to become a good enough parent to a Black child.

ACTION POINT

STRENGTHEN YOUR BONDS

This chapter's action point is focused on strengthening attachment in the family. Connection and solid bonds act as protection from toxic environments. They also communicate to us that we are worthy of love, care, and attention and encourage a child to feel safe enough to come to you with their distress.

We can all improve the quality of our bonds if we commit ourselves to doing so. Connection relies first and foremost on making time for bonding. It relies on seeing and hearing the Other and tapping into our capacity to show compassion to one another, including toward children. Human touch, eye contact, and active listening help most children feel contained. Make a connection action plan with your children, niblings, and other little humans around. Ensure that you regularly engage with the focus of connecting and making them feel heard and seen.

CHAPTER 6

WORKING WHILE BLACK

Case study: Sara

Sara is a Black British woman of Caribbean heritage in her early thirties who works as a manager in the civil service. Sara had been experiencing severe anxiety, debilitating shame, and difficulties working with her manager. Sara's manager is a white man, and she seemed to have developed a "phobic" response toward or extreme fear of him. Sara frequently found herself advocating for less-senior employees of color who faced discrimination. This added much tension in her relationship with management. She essentially became the voice of racism, thus the "troublemaker." She was treated with hostility and regularly covertly disrespected. Sara was finding the workplace increasingly oppressive and often ended up in tears. She was hopeless and overwhelmed when I spoke with her during an assessment. Exploring the relationship between Sara and her manager and the workplace as a structure formed a significant part of our work together. Of note, Sara had a history of being bullied, including racial harassment in her childhood, and had been the caregiver for her widowed father, as he spent most of her life in and out of severe depression.

We know that all organizations nowadays take equality "very seriously." Yet we also know that Sara's experience is far from uncommon. In fact, I have yet to meet a single Black employee who has not faced backlash for speaking out against racism.

To understand the lived experience of working while Black, various less-discussed manifestations of anti-Blackness will be explored and linked to some of the themes we have been grappling with so far. Black experiences at work cannot be separated from historical contexts. We therefore need to revisit the relationship between white spaces and Black bodies. These links will help us better appreciate some of the risks we commonly face and the strategies we can put in place to mitigate them. In this chapter we aim to make connections and reflect on common experiences of working while Black, and also how the injustices and injuries that can be sustained in the workplace not only mirror wider social inequality but also histories of trauma.

The "diversity and inclusion" industry—if not the diversity and inclusion industrial complex—is worth billions. In the US alone, companies spend over $8 billion on D&I training each year.[1] While a fortune is spent on "diversity and inclusion," Black graduates are still significantly less likely to find full-time jobs after graduating.[2] A recent study found that among young people in the UK who left university in 2017–18, 53 percent of the Black graduates had secured full-time employment, compared with 62 percent of white graduates.[3] What's more, a study by the Trade Union Congress found that they get paid 23 percent less than white graduates when they do find employment, and this gap widens as qualification increases.[4] The list of inequalities is long and, it would almost appear, never-ending. Inequalities at the point of access, inequalities in relation to progress, and inequalities in relation to discipline, to name but a few.

In all Western nations where data is collected, Black people continue to experience hostile workplaces. These structural injustices are not reducing; in fact, in some places they are getting worse.[5] While all this structural context is known, what is less understood is the lived reality of negotiating it, the more subtle and complex dynamics that can reproduce the wider system and how the Black body is treated in white workplaces.

The D&I industry's love affair with **unconscious bias** has done extraordinarily little to make workplaces less discriminatory places for Black people. It is arguably doing more harm than good by taking the focus away from structural racism and more complex unconscious dynamics. So, I am starting this chapter with three premises. First, that workplaces are a microcosm of society and that every dynamic and process that occurs between and within groups in society will get mirrored in institutions. Second, that organizations as organisms generally do not want to change and will resist change in various and elaborate ways, regardless of what they may tell themselves. A Black body inhabiting a previously all-white space is a fundamental change that can be and often will be resisted in various ways, some more obvious than others. The final premise is related to the first two premises, and it is that there is a level of communication, which is unseen and unconscious or preverbal, that neither Black employees nor white employers nor structures are adequately equipped for or willing to explore. It is often at this level of interaction that most race-related conflicts, tensions, and difficulties arise between Black employees and white institutions.

THE BLACK BODY AT WORK

Experiences of racism at work usually revolve around a main trope or script. The story often sounds like "one of those stories" you have heard many times before, and it usually has a strong déjà vu quality. This déjà vu quality is there because these experiences evoke past events and configurations and therefore need a historical lens to be understood. As we have seen, colonialism is the antithesis of personal sovereignty and boundary. I have therefore used the term "micro-colonialism" to refer to the everyday intrusions and breaches of boundaries, physical or psychological, such as invasions of privacy or personal space, that Black people continue to experience in white spaces, particularly from white men but not exclusively from them. These experiences are also gendered and subject to intersectional considerations. For example, one common gendered boundary violation concerns the policing of Black hair.

Case study: Black hair

In 2019, Lettia McNickle of Quebec successfully sued her employer Madisons New York Bar and Grill after being told to leave work because she was wearing braids. The restaurant was ordered to pay $14,500 in damages.[6]

There are plenty of examples of Black people in North America, particularly Black women, being punished for refusing to assimilate into whiteness via their hair. These assimilation orders are often rationalized under the guise of professionalism and uniform and grooming policies at work. Celebrities like Gabrielle Union have shared their experience of having their hair policed in the entertainment industry and being told that their hair was "too Black" for a show or a particular audience. But this is not a showbiz-specific issue. Nor is it an issue that only affects Black (North) Americans.

In the UK, cases of Black women being excluded or suspended from work on the basis of their hair frequently make the headlines too. In 2017, a Black woman alleged that she was told while applying for a job at Harrods that she would be required to relax, which is to chemically straighten, her hair, in order to be accepted for employment in the UK luxury store. The case ended up in front of UK parliamentarians. There is no specific legislation in the UK banning hair discrimination, although there have been successful litigated cases linking hair to either race or religious belief. There is limited protection throughout the Western world from hair discrimination.

The CROWN (Creating a Respectful and Open Workplace for Natural Hair) Act was added to the California Education Code and the Fair Employment and Housing Act in 2019. On top of accepting a definition of race that includes traits associated with a particular racial group, including hair texture and hairstyles, it rendered hair discrimination unlawful. California is the first state to ban discrimination against natural Black hairstyles such as cornrows, Afros, braids, and dreadlocks.

Although it has since been adopted beyond California, the CROWN Act is one of the very few legal protection frameworks that exist in the world to protect against discrimination on the grounds of hair. This is even though we know Black people and particularly Black women continue to face stereotypes, exclusion, and discipline because of the hair that grows out of their head. We now have evidence that wearing "natural" hairstyles leads to perception of lack of professionalism, and there are high penalties in terms of job opportunities for those who refuse to straighten their hair or style it in a way that makes it look as close to "European" hair as possible.[7]

Black women's hair texture and style continues to attract uninvited curiosity and intrusive questions, gazes, and touch.[8] Although there is a tendency to trivialize such exoticization, the history of Black hair within white supremacy is deep and fiercely political. And again, it is a history we cannot separate from colonialism and imperialism. The texture of Afro hair, for example, was used as "justification" for the enslavement of Africans between the sixteenth and nineteenth centuries. When a white hand without our consent gets into our hair, it evokes the history of being objectified and bestialized that is reenacted. The history of the animal zoo, where our ancestors were paraded as exotic mammals or primates. The history of entitlement to the Black body and the associated breaches of boundary.

BEING "THE ONLY ONE"

To be a Black professional often means being the only one in meetings, departments, and sometimes whole organizations. High status roles and places of power in society remain overwhelmingly white.[9] Black people have not, by and large, benefited from diversity programs or at least nowhere near the same level as white women and other people of color have.[10] The road to leadership and a senior role is an arduous one and, if we get there, we must contend with the experience of being the only Black face around. It is interesting that when I reflect on my clinical work with professionals of color the experience of being the only one is usually the experience that carries the most distress or anguish, often beyond experiences of overt discrimination.

Being the only one carries significant psychological risks and can set off complex dynamics including that of the white gaze and scapegoating. The lack of racial representation is central to our experience in the workplace; not seeing oneself represented at work is thus a foundational experience for many of us. Beyond organizational loss in terms of talent and innovation, there is also a loss, and a sense of grief, for

Black workers. It often translates into individuals struggling with belonging and homeness, themes that as we have seen in chapter 2 are deeply evocative of historical trauma. White institutions may go out of their way to recruit "BME and Black candidates" or to attract "difference," but once such (racial) difference enters the workplace, if it does at all, the expectation is usually that it must dress itself in whiteness. This rule is as powerfully as it is silently enforced. It is that very rule that dictates that we must remain silent when subjected to racism, that we must adapt, that we must overlook microaggressions, and generally that we must keep white people comfortable.

THE IMPACT OF STEREOTYPES

In 1997, while assessing math performance, researcher Steven Spencer found that when women were exposed to messages indicating that women perform as well as men on the test, they scored similarly to men.[11] When they were not, they scored more poorly on average than men. A few years later, similar results were found when assessing Black American students.[12] Black students who were exposed to negative stereotypes about intelligence, for example, performed worse than those who were not. Today we have many studies that document the same effect, and the dynamic has been given a name: stereotype threat.[13] There are various ways to make sense of these findings. Researchers have suggested that negative stereotypes lead those stereotyped to fear confirming the veracity of the feared stereotypes. To worry about their own performance, which might divert attention away from the task, compromising intellectual or cognitive performance. In that line of thought, stereotype threat is fear or anxiety of confirming stereotypes while taking a test.

There are, of course, various other ways to make sense of findings on stereotype threats, yet explanations for the phenomenon remain primarily theoretical. We may propose that we get discouraged or dispirited at being confronted with material that reminds us of racial injustice. Perhaps this affects our motivation to do well. We may also suggest that we identify with the stereotypes and therefore feel unconsciously pressured to act in accordance with them; this suggestion supports the dynamic of projective identification.

The impact of stereotypes on our cognitive or intellectual performance reminds us of how potent social forces can be in our psychological world and how such forces may come to influence how we are evaluated and/or how we respond to evaluation of our performances in work settings. Projective identification is an important dynamic for anyone serious about understanding race and the reproduction of inequality. Furthermore, it is a helpful tool for Black people to make sense of experiences we might have struggled to put into words. It provides us with a framework to take seriously our embodied responses in racialized exchanges and to consider what they might tell us about our personal sovereignty but also about our political sovereignty.

IMPOSTER SYNDROME

In this context is it not obvious that many of us would struggle with self-doubt and confidence when it comes to our competence? Or that we may come to experience imposter syndrome? **Imposterism or imposter syndrome** has been taken to refer to internal feelings of fraudulence or incompetence.[14] Those who are said to experience imposter syndrome perceive themselves to be less deserving of their achievements or roles and believe that others overestimate their abilities. Because of this discrepancy in terms of how they view themselves and how they are viewed by others, sufferers fear being discovered as a fraud. Although the original research on the phenomenon focused on white women, we now know that Black people face unique stressors and that, again, racial stereotypes lie at the center of their experiences. The lack of racial representation can activate internalized racism, which alone is associated with poor self-esteem and lack of confidence.

Assimilation for us is a complex process. Of course, there is a level of assimilation in the workplace that every employee regardless of their race and ethnicity must accept. Beyond this, there is, for Black employees, an additional level of labor that often goes unrecognized and is completely normalized. Another level of assimilation is racial and cultural—it's the expectation that Black people leave their Blackness at the door to get in, that they whiten themselves to be accepted by their peers or to not face barriers in relation to promotion.

This sort of assimilation is all-encompassing. It includes (but also goes far beyond) how our hair is worn. It includes not discussing our lived experience (particularly that of racism) and adopting modes of communication that may be alien to us to get ahead. So powerful is the expectation that we must leave our Blackness behind that many of us adopt a whole different persona, mannerisms, accent, and sometimes language to fit in at work, a process many refer to as "code switching." The term was coined by US sociolinguist John J. Gumperz to refer to polyglots switching between languages and ended up being applied to how Black Americans learn to switch from **African American Vernacular English (AAVE)** to standard English. Imagine going to work and having taught yourself for years, if not decades, to lead such an inauthentic life and fear being found out. Imagine the emotional demand, the exhaustion and alienation. Many of us do not have to imagine.

EXCELLENCE, EXHAUSTION, AND RESPECTABILITY

Many of us grow up in households where narratives such as "work harder" and "be smarter" are repeatedly enacted. "You have to be twice as good." Twice as good as everyone else and certainly twice as good as your white equivalent to simply be deemed good enough to stand underneath them. There is no doubt that part of these narratives originates from racial trauma and our intergenerational baggage. Still, our parents were not entirely incorrect. There is plenty of evidence that suggests that Black people, regardless of our sector, are more likely to be bypassed for promotion or recruitment even when they are the stronger candidates. The strategy of working twice as hard has heavy costs for our physical and mental health, as we have seen. It can lead to perfectionism, anxiety, and burnout. This is because the strategy of working twice as hard can increase our vulnerability to a kind of stress that psychologists sometimes refer to as **goal-striving stress.**

Goal-striving stress is occasioned by the discrepancy that exists between aspirations and achievement, particularly when our constant
striving to achieve does not lead to the outcome we seek. Research
indicates that goal-striving stress is associated with lower levels of happiness, life satisfaction, and self-esteem and higher levels of psychological distress.[15]

This same process has been termed "**John Henryism**." The empir-
ically documented health impact of "high-effort coping" we sometimes
put in place to attempt to overcome racial adversity and structural
racism has been linked to increased risks of cardiovascular disease,
heart attacks, and chronic health problems in Black groups.[16] **Black
excellence** peddles incessant goal-striving, the idea of working extra
hard and using any means necessary to "make it." It is the "die rich or
die trying" mentality, which is fundamentally tyrannical. We cannot
work our way out of white supremacy. We cannot excel our way out
of racism. The pressure that keeps us striving to do so is racism. Black
excellence is a rebranding of **respectability politics**, the idea that emulating white middle-class values, presentation, and culture can "uplift
the race" and eliminate caricatures of Blackness as intellectually deficient, doomed to eternal poverty and illiteracy. This aspiration to Black
exceptionalism fails to consider classist and capitalistic thinking and
cannot be separated from racist logic. Emulating the master's politics
reifies the master's superiority and their contempt for Blackness.

SUMMARY

1.

The historical load that the Black body carries is almost impossible to escape from, and this history gets reproduced at work. It can manifest in the extra scrutiny Black bodies attract from bosses and peers and the difficulties we experience being accepted within white spaces.

2.

Stereotypes, projections, and projective identification all colliding can lead to unfair and biased performance appraisals. More significantly, they can challenge the boundaries of our minds and lead to us enacting negative expectations.

3.

Control or surveillance measures in the workplace and in white spaces cannot be separated from control and surveillance measures in the broader sociopolitical context (in the same way we have argued that sociopolitical sovereignty cannot be separated from personal sovereignty).

4.

The lived experience of working while Black is complex, and it continues to be, for far too many of us, a story of exclusion, a story of exhaustion, and a story of alienation that can lead to distress and racial trauma.

....

In the next chapter, "Black Love," we will consider the impact of racism on intimate and romantic relationships and the ways racism can shape how we love and who we love.

RACE REFLECTIONS

To understand the experience of working while Black it is necessary to connect past and present to recognize relational patterns that continue to lead to exclusion, marginalization, and Othering. This section gives you the opportunity to reflect and develop skills to help resist and navigate the workplace and help protect your body and mind.

What have you found most troubling in this chapter?

You may want to explore your physical responses and the images and thoughts that came to you and explore what they might take you back to. Please use the Race Reflections reflective model (p. 183) to help you.

_____

_____

_____

_____

_____

What key obstacles have you faced in your career, and what strategies have you built to navigate them?

Assessing the reality of what working while Black has meant can be scary and uncomfortable, but it is not possible to plan resistance and self-care strategies without contemplating the challenge. Please make a list of these challenges.

_____

_____

_____

_____

_____

> Thinking of ourselves outside of work achievements helps
> build an independent identity so we aren't only dependent
> on work outcomes for life satisfaction.

Who you are is not determined by others' ability to recognize your abilities. You are much more than your work or job title. What are the things that matter to you? What are your values? What kind of contribution do you want to make to the world?

_____

_____

_____

_____

_____

> We have seen that the same politics at a national or geopolitical
> level shapes how the Black body is treated and how breaches
> of boundaries occur frequently and threaten our bodily and
> psychological autonomy and sovereignty.

Take time to consider your boundaries and see whether you do all you can to protect yourself from intrusion at work. What expectations exist where you work that may put you at risk? What stereotypes do you fear confirming? How might you hold on to your sense of identity (including your talents and aptitudes) at work?

_____

_____

_____

_____

_____

ACTION POINT

STRATEGIZE

One of the most helpful actions you can take when it comes to navigating the workplace while Black is to have an overall strategy about how you are going to maximize the chance of you achieving your career goals. This strategy must consider race-based challenges you are likely to face on your way and tools and resources you can draw from to attempt to overcome them. The point here is not to create an illusion that what we achieve at work is only within our control; it is not. Rather, it is to have a plan, to be prepared psychologically and practically.

Your action point: You have spent some time reflecting on common challenges and on the challenges you have faced. Now make a list of all the resources you turn to for support. These may include

- identifying allies (particularly those in positions of seniority) in and outside the workplace and, if possible, getting one of them to mentor you

- getting to know and considering joining support structures that may exist to protect your rights (e.g., unions, Black employee groups)

- developing a side hustle to increase your options, financial autonomy, and confidence

- maintaining relationships with colleagues and bosses who have been supportive

- seeking others who may share your experience to combat isolation and marginalization

Once you have that list, take steps to make sure that these support systems are accessible. This will entail ensuring that contact and communication is established and maintained so these resources may be ready to use when you need them.

CHAPTER 7

BLACK LOVE

I grew up never seeing a doll that looked like me. When I was a child, Black dolls were unheard of in France. Even today they are still hard to find in mainstream stores. To this day, if I happen to be in a store that sells Black dolls (the darker the better), I find it hard to resist buying them and marveling at them. Like many French Black people of my generation who are mildly socially conscious and grew up with no Black dolls, before becoming a parent I had fantasies about buying lots of Black dolls for my unborn child. A cousin fulfilled that fantasy. She bought her daughter a Black doll a few years ago for her birthday. She waited anxiously, anticipating her daughter's reaction as she unwrapped the present. Instead of joy, sadness, tears, and a temper tantrum followed. "Why would you buy me an ugly doll?" she cried. Her mother's jaw dropped. She had not seen this coming. There was nothing unusual in the doll's appearance. In fact, you could argue there was nothing remotely Black about it as far as features went, if you looked carefully. She even had waist-length straight brown hair. But the source of the young child's distress was that she had picked up the notion that lighter was prettier. That Black doll was ugly, and she was inconsolable.

This book started by centering love as an antidote to racial trauma. Radical love. The politics of Black love are complex, and Black love, arguably like all matters pertaining to Blackness, is a political issue. Historically, Black people have been taught to see each other with disdain and suspicion. To see ourselves as undesirable and unworthy of love and care. These notions can only be fully understood if we situate them in a framework of interlocking systems of oppression: racism, classism, and sexism. In this chapter we explore the complexities of Black love, revisit internalized racism, and propose tools and strategies to heal our often deeply wounded relationships.

THE CONTEXT OF LOVE

Psychologists Kenneth and Mamie Clark had already discovered that children favor white dolls over seventy years ago.[1] Their famous "doll tests," experiments that aimed to document the psychological effects of segregation on African American children, found that both Black and white children preferred white dolls when given the choice between two dolls differing only in skin tone. More worryingly, when asked to explain their choice, children as young as three ascribed negative attributes to Black dolls, such as meanness, laziness, and ugliness. The 253 children who participated in the study were ages three to seven. These children had already learned that white was right. The Clarks' study contributed to the ending of school segregation in the United States as it gave evidence that segregation created feelings of inferiority in Black children and affected their psychological health. Clearly the story of my niece in the mid-2010s, in France, a child who has never known legal segregation, shows the reach of this phenomenon. The research has been replicated inside and outside the US, sometimes with different results but often with the same.

Attractiveness plays a fundamental role in the social allocation of resources that include material resources and power. Research has shown that those deemed attractive tend to do better structurally.[2] They are also more sought after romantically. We cannot talk with honesty about love and loving relationships without speaking about attractiveness. And who we deem attractive we treat more favorably. When it comes to criteria for women's attractiveness, constructions of beauty and femininity are intrinsically linked, and such constructions have always been central to systems of domination and marginalization. It is not coincidental that "low-rank" women (and people more generally) have been socially constructed as less desirable. So the alleged lack of femininity of disabled women, trans women, poor women, elderly women, and women of color, especially dark-skinned Black women, continues to be used to dehumanize us. To keep us at the margins of society and justify the violence we experience.

INTERRACIAL LOVE

I want to consider interracial relationships at this juncture. No doubt many may be tempted to interrogate this decision. The stereotype of the bitter and angry Black woman comes to mind. It is a device often employed when we attempt to explore the impact of white supremacy in romantic relationships. And a device often intended to stop us from investigating social issues that deeply impact our lives.[3] If you are curious about where I stand, in the interest of transparency, I will say this: I have nothing against interracial relationships of any configurations. Attempting to legislate love and physical attraction is the epitome of human futility. Nonetheless, this should not stop us from contextualizing such relationships and exploring mixed relationships as a rich site for exploration of both inter- and intra-group race relations, which can therefore help us understand the complexities of racial trauma and intergenerational wounds.[4]

According to the 2011 UK census, 9 percent of people in a relationship were in an interethnic relationship in England and Wales.[5] This had increased from 7 percent in 2001. Of note, "Other Black" (62 percent) comprised the group (non-mixed/multiple) that was the second-most likely to be in an interracial relationship. White Brits were least likely to be in interethnic relationships (4 percent), followed by Bangladeshis (7 percent), Pakistanis (9 percent), and Indians (12 percent). Of all people in interethnic relationships, 40 percent included someone who was white British. In the US, the picture is strikingly dissimilar.[6] Overall, the most common type of interracial marriage is between white and Hispanic (of all races), which accounted for 38 percent of all interracial marriages in 2010. White-Asian couples accounted for another 14 percent of interracial marriages, and white-Black couples made up 8 percent. In both countries, Black men are much more likely to be in interracial relationships than Black women.

The patterns call for some reflection. Why such a discrepancy? Why are interracial relationships not shared equally between the genders in Black groups? One key difference between the UK and US contexts is the legal history of interracial relationships. Miscegenation or the "interbreeding" of people considered to be of different racial groups was unlawful for most of US history. It was only fully legalized in 1967.[7] Various fears underpinned this social taboo, including the politics of eugenics and racial purity and fantasized threats to one's nation's health, bloodline, and security, to name a few. Black races constructed as morally, genetically, and intellectually inferior needed to be kept away from the white genetic pool in order to protect white supremacy and the social order as evidenced by the "one drop rule." The one drop rule is the racial classification principle that dictated that if anyone, no matter what they look like, had a known Black ancestor, that person would automatically be classified as Black.[8]

The fear of whiteness being contaminated by Blackness also reflected a deep fear of being outnumbered by Black people in the colonies, where white settlers were long the minority. Policing love has always been policing the boundaries of power. What is more, the possibility that Black Americans carry in their consciousness and with more vivacity the sexual horrors carried out on American soil cannot be discounted. Amid miscegenation fantasies, there is ample evidence that rape was a central feature of slavery. A legacy that means, today, that genetic databases suggest that, on average, 24 percent of the Black American gene pool can be traced back to European ancestry. Of course, the rape of slaves and of colonial subjects was a common practice across the Americas, including the Caribbean and colonized Africa, and thus affected the racial composition in the West Indies and to a much lesser extent in African colonies. Some may argue that this is a history Black Brits can more easily disconnect from because the sexual horrors were not primarily carried out on Britain's soil. This allowed some distancing from that historical violence. But if we consider that loving Black-white relationships in the US and UK disproportionately involve a Black man, perhaps the sexual atrocities carried out on Black women's bodies and the associated trauma also play a part in how Black women relate to white men, among other factors. Perhaps there is a taboo that is still alive.

MISOGYNOIR: WHEN RACISM IS GENDERED OR SEXISM IS RACIALIZED

The term "misogynoir" is an application of intersectional thinking. Coined by Black feminist scholar and cultural theorist Moya Bailey, it seeks to describe, per Dictionary.com, "the specific hatred, dislike, distrust, and prejudice directed toward Black women" and provides a framework to explore how misogyny intersects with anti-Black racism and leads to patterns of harm uniquely affecting Black women. The devaluation of Black women's bodies is alive and well. I remember when, in May 2011, *Psychology Today* published an article by UK-based evolutionary psychologist Satoshi Kanazawa titled "Why Are Black Women Less Physically Attractive Than Other Women?" The article was met with mass outrage.[9] It made several claims, including that "black women are objectively less physically attractive than nonblack women" yet "subjectively consider themselves to be far more physically attractive than others." In the news, we continue to see Black politicians and public figures called ugly, bestialized (compared to animals), and denigrated because of their appearance.

Black people's bodies have long been consumed yet devaluated under the institutions of colonialism and slavery. Especially the Black female body. This body was not only viewed as inferior in intelligence and sophistication and as being lower down the chain of evolution; it was also ugly, abnormal, animalistic, hypersexual, athletic, and masculine. The promotion of white-cis-hetero patriarchy has been central to the colonial construction of femininity. It places at opposite poles Black and white women, with purity, grace, and beauty arbitrarily accorded to white women—and depravity, bestiality, and androgyny fixed onto constructions of Black womanhood. This is done to bolster a European aesthetic and thus white womanhood. Nowhere is the arbitrariness of these constructions more observable than when white women and other women of color receive praise and admiration for features typically devalued in Black women.[10] This tells us three things: First, the concept of beauty is arbitrary, at least to a large extent. Second, the constructed beauty of specific features is very much dependent on who carries them. Finally, beauty is fundamentally linked to power.

In 2000, American feminist theorist and academic Patricia Hill Collins called dominant stereotypes of Black women "controlling images."[11] These have been used through time to restrict Black women's freedom, exercise social control, and maintain white capitalist patriarchal interests. Those stereotypes have their origin in Hill Collins's study of Black American representation over the ages. They reveal intersections of systems of race, gender, and class oppression and their role in the distribution of material resources and in the politics of love, which can illuminate the complexities of fostering Black love within white supremacy. Each of them reflects white supremacy's vested interests in keeping Black women subservient. The stereotypes include the four described below.

The mammy

The stereotype of the mammy is the portrayal of the Black woman as obedient and dedicated to caring for her white master and his family. The mammy is a docile domestic servant, who derives pleasure from completing domestic chores and looking after white children. The mammy image is the social expectation when it comes to Black womanhood. She is the good Black woman. Nurturing, content in servitude, and committed to the welfare of white folks, she sacrifices her own needs for the needs of the white family. Hill Collins argues that the mammy trope symbolizes the dominant group's fear of Black women's sexuality.

The matriarch

The matriarch is the dominant, aggressive, and overbearing Black woman. She is a failed mother. She is a failed wife too. The matriarch "emasculates" Black men and drives them away. The matriarch is essentially a failed mammy. She works way too hard and away from home, which takes her away from her children, which is seen as neglectful. It is the alleged neglect by Black matriarchs that supposedly leads to poor behavior, poor educational achievements, crimes in Black communities, and the fractures that exist in Black families.

The welfare mother

The welfare mother is characterized by her inability to stop procreating. She has children she cannot afford and is dependent on the state and is therefore the cause of her own poverty. She is to blame for the poverty in Black American communities. The welfare mother's unrestrained capacity to produce more Black children speaks of a deep fear of being taken over and outnumbered by Black people. But it also speaks of the presumed lack of morality and responsibility of Black women.

The Jezebel

The final controlling image is the Jezebel, who is all about sexual aggression and "promiscuity." She is the forever-horny Black woman who exists for the sexual satisfaction of men. This image is deeply linked to slavery's construction of Black women as dangerous temptresses who could lure white men away from saintly Christ-approved sex with white women. The Jezebel stereotype hyper-sexualizes Black women and affords them magic sexual powers over men. The stereotype was, of course, handy to justify the sexual abuse, rape, and exploitation of Black women by both Black and white men.

....

What these tropes also lay bare is wishful revisioning of history via projection. They allow Black women to be held responsible for the success or failure of romantic relationships in Black communities. As such, they bear much relevance to Black womanhood over the diaspora. Everyday language used to stereotype Black women in Britain—such as bossy, fierce, controlling, bullish, fiery, lazy, and slutty—neatly maps onto Hill Collins's analysis.

In her hard-hitting essay published in 2013, which gave birth to a chapter in her book *Don't Touch My Hair*, Irish historian Emma Dabiri examines the lack of visibility and erasure of Black women in representations of mainstream Black British culture.[12] Such is the erasure that you would be "forgiven for thinking we are an endangered species," she writes. She notes that Black men and white women dominate representations of love in the British media, which calls attention to the enduring taboo around this social phenomenon. Dabiri also references the controlling images to make sense of the exclusion of Black women in British media. She suggests that this ensures their gendered and racial subordination, and she sees them facing rejection and denigration from those Black men who aspire to be in relationships with more socially valued women. Women whose aesthetics are judged to be superior, even in the eyes of Black men and those of their peers.

There is no doubt that systemic racism harms Black family structures. In the US in the 1920s, 90 percent of Black children were born to married parents. That ratio was 80 percent by the late 1950s, and it is about 20 percent today.[13] These numbers portray contemporary difficulties with Black love in the US. Black men are vulnerable to being removed from their communities because of structural injustices and enduring social inequalities.[14] This means that Black women have advanced at a faster rate in education and the job market. This gendered difference in socioeconomic positioning can further fuel tension as it echoes historical scripts and trauma around wounded manhood and men's impaired capacity to protect their partners and family in Black groups, still an enduring gendered social expectation in **cisgendered heterosexual (cishet)** relationships.

Black women are not exempt from internalizing systems of oppression, including white patriarchy and classism. It is difficult to imagine that Black men's reduced capacity to offer material protection to Black women and access structures of power would play zero role in how we relate. Still, extraordinarily little is known about this reciprocal dynamic and how it leads to the performance of Black love.

Again, in terms of intergenerational context, enslaved Black men were commonly removed from their loved ones and communities.[15] Violated and humiliated in front of their partners and families. They also witnessed their families and partners being brutalized and raped. This context, many believe, has created difficulties in lasting intimate relationships with men or women, difficulties that are made worse by disrupted attachments and bonds, as we have seen in chapter 4.

Case study: Alicia

The first time I met Alicia, my jaw almost dropped. She was truly one of the most striking women I had ever laid eyes on. Alicia was a queer Black woman in her early twenties, tall, dark, and statuesque, with perfectly drawn African features. She came to see me because she was feeling low and had a history of depression. She fought tears throughout most of our first session, self-conscious, it seemed, about being vulnerable in front of the total stranger I was. She complained about not liking herself very much. She had a history of sexually abusive relationships and was a serial dater of white people, mainly men. She struggled to get on romantically with Black people. She said she simply did not get their attention. As I observed her, almost unable to maintain eye contact with me, it was difficult to reconcile how she viewed herself with who I saw sitting in the chair in front of me. But this was not a performance, and it became obvious very quickly that this dysmorphic relationship Alicia had with her body was racialized. She hated her nose. She hated her lips. She was not fond of her skin. She informed me that she was the darkest person in her family. She repeated this a few times. People would stare at her, she would say to me, tearing up. She thought they stared because she was ugly or weird. And that something must be wrong with her. It took us almost two years for Alicia to start changing her relationship with her body, which coincided with her stopping dating white people exclusively.

There is a lot that has historical resonance when considering Alicia's story. We see in it a troubled relationship with her body and with her sexuality. We see too a troubled relationship with her color and racialized features. There are also important themes of abuse and invisibility. Alicia sought multiple sexual partners who were white, but she was aware there was something troubling in her relationship with white people. Alicia was dependent on their sexual attention to maintain the little self-esteem she had, yet every time she was ill-treated, her self-love plummeted. Still, the attraction to whiteness kept her in a vicious cycle of dependency.

Fanon perfectly articulated the desire for white sexual partners as the desire for whiteness.[16] For women, this desire cannot be separated from the need for material security and access to structures of power. Acceptance into high society or structures of power becomes a metaphor for being accepted into whiteness regardless of the psychological costs and loss of dignity. The complexity and poignancy of these words is that seeking white partners is a form of self-harm for Fanon, who questions whether love across the racial divide is attainable with Black inferiority and white superiority as constant. Fanon suggests that in this context authentic love is virtually impossible, as this positioning toward whiteness is born out of a need to defend ourselves against feelings of insignificance and a disowned need for white approval. Such impulses are therefore a call to turn white.

Racial whitening was an ideology common in South America and part of the Caribbean that attempted to bring Black people up the class hierarchy.[17] Racial whitening was therefore practiced to advance Black people culturally and genetically with support from scientific racism. We see echoes of internalized whiteness in Alicia's attempt to seek a sense of self-worth and validation from the white gaze, regardless of how abusive. This reproduced a cycle of relational self-harm that was bolstered by her self-hatred. But, similarly, we may be curious about the treatment she has experienced at the hands of Black people. Once aware of the historical issues we have covered, we can better resist the repetition of history.

LOVE AT THE INTERSECTIONS

Finding love and sustaining love amid racism is not the complete story. We have seen how racism, sexism, and classism bear strong influence on Black love. Many of us must also deal with homophobia, ableism, and other axes of oppression, their intersections, and the additional challenges they bring to already complex terrain. Multiple marginalized identities can be highly stigmatized within Black communities.[18] Part of this stigma is a residue of the intergenerational context. For example, many countries in Africa still have homophobic laws put into effect by European colonizers.[19] Black immigrants would have come from cultures or countries where homosexuality is simply socially unacceptable and in some places carries the risk of state-sanctioned death. In the Caribbean, the taboo of homosexuality has, in part, been linked to the rape or torture of male slaves.[20] Across the diaspora the legacy of medical racism can manifest in disabled people bringing "shame" onto the "Black race" and evidence of our inhumanity.

Much of the stigma here is likely related to the politics of respectability and our collective internalization of inferiority. It is not a surprise that those located at the intersections of axes of oppression will have qualitatively different experiences of Black love and intimacy. Many of us experience a sense of being doubly or triply unlovable, doubly or triply excluded from intimacy. These multilayered experiences of Otherness heighten experiences of isolation, which can compound unsafeness and make it hard to trust in relationships. In the case of queer love, for example, for many in our community it is not safe to live one's love openly. This means feeling unsafe and unwelcome because of queer/homo/bi/transphobia and finding no refuge in white society, including mainstream LGBTQIA+ spaces, because of anti-Blackness. And this means losing ties to one's heritage and cultural home and thus support networks and traditions that many depend on for well-being, security, and belonging.

As a result, LGBTQIA+ Black people are at high risk of psychological distress, self-harm, and suicide, and many continue to be at significant risk of harm.[21] In terms of love, the lack of social support can translate into the pressure to stay in relationships that may be abusive or unfulfilling due to fear of being alone and losing another source of support, a tangible lived reality. Furthermore, much of what we know about functioning in relationships we learn from observing relationships around us, particularly that of our parents and images in the media. There are additional challenges for our queer siblings. The lack of representation of queer Black love further limits access to appropriate role models when it comes to navigating multiple traumas and maintaining loving relationships.

Still, there are reasons to be hopeful. Objection to narrow, heteronormative, white-dominated love is mounting across the globe. Stories, images, and representations of love we have been excluded from are becoming accessible, allowing those who have had to live their love in the shadows for too long to take space with pride. There is a new generation engaged in addressing intergenerational trauma and seeking help. Therapy, for example, appears to be losing its taboo. We are talking more and are increasingly aware of what we have inherited and what we're choosing to leave behind.

Younger generations are challenging what love means and what relationships should look like, contesting Eurocentric notions of love.

In the UK, a coalition of public figures, such as model Jourdan Dunn, presenter Clara Amfo, Team GB boxer Nicola Adams, journalist Yomi Adegoke, and spoken-word artist George the Poet have come together to launch a campaign to make Black love more visible and inclusive. #MyLoveIsBlackLove aims to showcase Black love in its multitude and to be more representative of what Black love looks like in Britain today. Finally, Busy Being Black, a compendium of queer Black voices, is gaining prominence. It showcases an oral history project and a podcast centering "those who have learnt—and are learning—to thrive at the intersections of their identities." Busy Being Black, like so many coalitions of Black queer love, is all about challenging narrow, heteronormative, white-dominated love. And so, stories, images, and representations of love we have been deprived of are becoming accessible, if not center stage. The future of Black love is looking bright and rainbow.

SUMMARY

1.

There are many challenges associated with Black love. They are better understood by locating them in a historical and intergenerational context.

2.

Constructions of beauty and attractiveness, which play a fundamental role in the social allocation of resources and power and femininity, have traditionally excluded the Black female body.

3.

Interlocking systems of oppression make seeing each other as we are an ongoing challenge.

4.

Enduring social inequality and experiences of racism that are mediated by gendered stereotypes and cisgendered heterosexual norms put stress and strain on our intimate relationships, particularly for those whose Blackness meets queerness.

....

In the next and final chapter, "Black Resistance," we contextualize our long history of defiance and insurgency and look at tools that can help us thrive and resist white supremacy.

RACE REFLECTIONS

Our intimate and romantic relationships are not exempt from the influence of racism and racial trauma. Given how vital our close bonds are in terms of support, connection, and welfare, it is vitally important that we invest as much as we can to attempt to heal the wounds of racial trauma. This section gives you the opportunity to reflect on love and intimacy.

What have you found most troubling in this chapter?

You may want to explore your bodily responses and the images and thoughts that came to you and explore what they might take you back to. Please use the Race Reflections reflective model (p. 183) to help you.

_____

_____

_____

_____

_____

Maintaining love for one another amid structural racism can be a minefield, but that Black love is fundamental to our wellness and resistance.

What are the key challenges you faced in your romantic relationships, and what strategies have you built to overcome them? Knowing what you now know, what would you do differently?

_____

_____

_____

_____

_____

Our earlier relationships and romantic role models
can affect how we relate to partners.

*Watching your parents and those around you, who do you want to carry
with you, and who do you want to leave behind as you move forward? Who
are your role models when it comes to love and specifically Black love? Take
time to consider racism, sexism, and other axes of oppression.*

_____

_____

_____

_____

_____

Images and gendered and/or racialized stereotypes deeply affect
how we see and treat one another romantically, making it challenging
to see ourselves for who we are. Reevaluate any problematic
notions centering love and compassion.

*Take time to consider what racism has taught you about people of different
genders that might be negatively impacting your intimate relationship(s)
and how you might have in the past reacted as a result.*

_____

_____

_____

_____

_____

ACTION POINT

MAKE A LOVE PLEDGE

I sometimes say that showing love loudly and deliberately is necessary to counterbalance the covert and overt hatred that Blackness attracts. Think about it: We live in a world where we are much more likely to see Black bodies brutalized or policed in public than we are to see them being loved unapologetically at school gates, on the streets, or on our screens. Remedying this unbalance is a political act. But it is likely also a public health matter. We need to show one another unconditional love and to do so without restraint or reservations, to reclaim our humanity.

Your action point: You are therefore invited to make a love pledge. To show love consciously and deliberately to Black people, to leave those who matter to you in no doubt about your love for them. Think about how you show love to those close to you and to those around you. Ask those you are intimate with how you can love them better and tell them how they can help you feel loved, then commit to loving one another better.

CHAPTER 8

BLACK RESISTANCE

Some of my earliest memories in mental health wards have stayed with me. I cherish them. They have truly shaped me as a psychologist. One such experience happened early in my career, about fifteen years ago, in London. A psychologist, who was a woman of color, complained to me about Black patients she had been allocated to work with. This was as part of a specific service available to Black people. Frustrated, she moaned: "It's impossible to work with these patients, they're stuck on racism." Then she casually walked away, angry, leaving me puzzled. It took several years for me to even come close to grasping the racism contained in this simple statement and the history it laid bare. Revisiting this experience now triggers anger in me. It would be impossible to grasp the violence of this exchange without looking once more at history. In this chapter, we consider Black resistance. We have covered a lot of ground in *Living While Black* and thought a lot about living and surviving. It is important that we remember that the only reason we are here is because of our history of resistance. Our history of wanting better. Our history of continuing to believe that, despite all odds, freedom is possible.

In this chapter we consider what Black resistance might look like today and some of the tools we may use not only to live but to thrive while Black.

THE PATHOLOGIZATION OF BLACK RESISTANCE

"Drapetomania" and "rascality"

"Drapetomania" was believed to be an inheritable but preventable "mental illness" that caused enslaved Africans to run away and flee captivity, often repeatedly and always against their best interests. Their best interests, of course, being dutifully serving their white master—bending the knee. "Rascality," scientifically known as dysesthesia aethiopica, on the other hand, was said to be a disease of the mind characterized by laziness, defiance, lack of work ethic, and mischievous behavior. This mischief was clear. It was always related to indifference and disregard of the interests of the master if not outright sabotage. Contrary to drapetomania, rascality, it was asserted, could helpfully be recognized by clear physical symptoms that were visible. Marks and lesions on the back of the sufferer, for example, showcased not only their insensitive skin but also their diseased mind. Such mental illnesses were so serious and communicable that they led to countless rebellions, including the liberation of Haiti. Thus, they instilled fear in the hearts of white slave owners.

This historical context reminds us that medicine and mental health disciplines such as psychiatry have long histories of racism.[1] But, more than that, it tells us something of critical significance about the role that the "sciences of the mind" have played in the production and re-production of the dominant values of society and how deeply invested in the maintenance of the racialized social order they have been. We can also see that the practice of silencing Black people—their social realities however violent, however unjust, however torturous, however traumatic—has been normative and that those seeking to challenge or change unequal structures have always been at risk of pathologization and violence in health systems.

Even though Black people have been pathologized for resisting oppression, we have never been passive recipients of racist violence. As we will explore, there is a long-documented history of Black resistance dating as far back as the earliest encounter on the African coastline. By resistance, I simply mean the process of opposing racism and race-based domination and working toward liberation. We resisted even when it meant inevitable death. It is within that struggle for resistance that we have continued to assert our humanity and right to exist free from racism. Resistance has also allowed us to keep our sanity even though it has made those set on refusing to see us as humans see us as insane.

FORMS OF RESISTANCE

Resistance has taken several forms. During the Middle Passage, uprisings and suicides were common. On plantations, resistance meant damaging the master's property or machinery or running away despite the obvious risks. Clearly, drapetomania was contagious. It is that spirit of resistance that has ensured the survival of many of the cultural practices we can easily recognize across the diaspora. African customs, religious beliefs, names, and music were fundamental ways to resist the complete erasure of one's heritage and indoctrination into whiteness. This resistance has, of course, always attracted severe sanction, violence, or pathologization.

Nowhere is this truer than within the mental health system. My early experience on the ward in London may on the surface look quite different from the process by which Black people in southern plantations were diagnosed with drapetomania. Different until we consider the group who exasperated the psychologist, for being "stuck on racism," is part of a group of service users who have received some of the most adverse mental health "care" imaginable, as seen in chapter 2. Many had spoken about police officers sitting on their back during arrests or mental health staff restraining them to the point of broken bones. All had been deprived of their liberties. The violence they attempted to articulate and to process with someone whose job it is to primarily listen was disturbing too. Despite this, these vulnerable patients clearly in need of support for racial trauma and support in their resistance were, and continue to be, failed.

Today, subtler ways of pathologizing resistance can be found in and outside the mental health system. It is this pathologization that betrays the assumption that there is nothing worth protesting or worth changing in the unjust social order. And/or that psychological maturity is assessed by our capacity to accept and adapt to racial injustice—hence, why we should not name racism and certainly not seek to resist it. And why that resistance is pathological.

Psychological resistance

One of the most common dilemmas we must face and that I encounter clinically is whether to resist racism or accept it. Sometimes people conclude that they must choose their battles because constantly fighting against racism can be hazardous when the stuff is everywhere. There certainly is much truth to this. Although, once more, there are various ways to resist. I often remind people who come to see me and are anxious that they are not doing resistance right that we are all trying to figure out how to navigate racism. There is no magic formula. If there was, it would have been discovered by now. Racism is an animal that continually adapts and evolves and twists and turns. During such gymnastics, having a large repertoire of behavioral and psychological resistance strategies is necessary.

Yet, it is true too that some may think racism is just a part of life, and they may say they are scared to speak out. Let us address these issues in turn.

Researchers have examined coping mechanisms and responses to racism and their impact on trauma symptoms. In this kind of research, passive coping mechanisms such as accepting that there is nothing we can do about racism and active coping mechanisms (for example, organizing) are usually compared. Individuals who show an acceptance of race discrimination and who, for instance, tend to keep racism to themselves tend to report significantly higher levels of distress or trauma "symptoms" than those who name their experiences and challenge them.[2]

It is also true that our coping and resistance strategies often expose us to more racism. Speaking up or instigating formal complaints has been linked to further racism through retaliation from institutions or from those in a position of power increasing risks of racial trauma.[3]

Nonetheless more must be said about fear. White terror has long been used to terrorize those who sought to engage in resistance. There is a long history of torture, sadistic punishment, and grotesque murder of those who resisted racial oppression.[4] The infliction of torture and pain to dominate or control and thus protect white economic interests has reigned. Over time, there is little doubt that violence has left collective scars in the form of intergenerational fears of resistance within families. The passing down of acceptance and silence to survive.

Silence as resistance

The function, the profoundly serious function, of racism is distraction. It keeps you from doing your work. It keeps you explaining, repeatedly, your reason for being. Somebody says you have no language, and you spend twenty years proving that you do. Somebody says your head is not shaped properly so you have scientists working on the fact that it is. Somebody says you have no art, so you dredge that up. Somebody says you have no kingdoms, so you dredge that up. None of this is necessary. There will always be one more thing.

—Toni Morrison[5]

I have repeatedly said in this book that silence is often a consequence of trauma.[6] There is nonetheless one area where silence may be more adaptive. Silence as refusal to engage. Silence here is a form of psychological boundary and can be a powerful way to refuse to center whiteness and to debate our humanity. This is the reason I advocate nonengagement with white people who dispute matters related to white privilege, oppression, and racism. Let them be. Often this means letting them feel intellectually superior and comfortable in their uncritical notions of objectivity. Learning to unhook ourselves from this sadistic interaction is central to us keeping sufficient energy to focus on our liberation. The emotional labor of engaging in such debate is not worth it. And we need to recognize that there are simply too many more important things to do with our time and energy. Life is short. Why waste another single moment of it entertaining bigotry dressed as reason. Toni Morrison said this more eloquently than any of us ever could: "The function of racism is distraction." We cannot reason our way out of racism.

Engaging in debates is a waste of time. I repeat: engaging in debates is a waste of time. But more than a waste of time, it is psychologically taxing. Meaningful dialogue requires reciprocity, the willingness to treat the Other as an equal and to trust their experience. This is what engaging in good faith entails. White supremacy does not seek to engage in good faith—it seeks to maintain supremacy. It will twist, turn, and forever shift to maintain its superiority as you make yourself ill trying to prove you are being harmed. None of that is necessary. Making our existence and our lived reality subject to agreement, debate, or approval is maintaining power relations by making the existence of racism dependent on the approval or understanding of those who enact racism, those whose very sense of self depends on the erasure of the violence they enact. In this context, silence *is* resistance.

In this line of thought, author and journalist Reni Eddo-Lodge's *Why I'm No Longer Talking to White People About Race* made the point perfectly. She writes:

> I'm no longer engaging with white people on the topic of race. Not all white people, just the clear majority who refuse to accept the existence of structural racism and its symptoms. I can no longer engage with the gulf of an emotional disconnect that white people display when a person of colour articulates their experience. You can see their eyes shut down and harden. It is as if treacle is poured into their ears, blocking up their ear canals. It is like they can no longer hear us.[7]

Connecting as resistance

One of the reasons why racism inflicts trauma is because it forces us to disconnect. This disconnection increases in contexts of exclusion and marginalization. This cultural homelessness that so many of us must learn to be at home with is constantly triggered by everyday microaggressions and covert Othering messages. It is within this sense of homelessness that so much intergenerational trauma resonates and is carried through, beyond individualized coping and resistance strategies. There must therefore be community-level healing that nurtures the soul and strengthens our bonds. Racism causes us to disconnect at multiple levels. To disconnect from earth, soil, and our environment as adults by avoiding parks and places of greenery for fear of being reported to the police and seen as trespassers. Or when we simply live way too far from them due to environmental or structural racism.

We disconnect from our heritage as we learn to internalize shame about the land, the customs of our forebears, and our histories. We disconnect from our minds and bodies because it is nearly impossible to feel at home within ourselves when we are constantly gaslighted and taught to distrust our embodied realities. And, finally, we disconnect from each other, too, as many of us come to be seduced by the thought of sitting at the master's table and reenacting exclusion and gatekeeping through that scarcity mentality that helps to ensure that those who look like us are barred from structures that few of us manage to access.

What does more harm to us than these multiple-level disconnections? Our ancestral heritage recognizes the importance of connection. Resistance must therefore focus on connecting with our body, mind, community, history, and the environment. African-centered conceptualizations of wellness are based on a symbiotic relationship with the world around us, including nature, earth, soil, and our ancestors. It is that mutual relationship that exists between living and nonliving entities that ensures harmony and continuation of the past into the present. From this non-Western perspective, connecting with the land connects us to memories but also to community and history. It is for this reason that I often suggest to those who return to their ancestral land that they connect with the earth there and bring some soil back with them.

Case study: Music as resistance

Marie is a Congolese woman seeking asylum in the UK. She is beautiful and in her early thirties. She has experienced and witnessed some of the ugliest violence humans are capable of inflicting on one another. She was tortured, held captive, and raped during war. Marie saw her son mutilated to death. She and I crossed paths in a detention center in the UK—she hardly spoke English or French. I could hardly speak Lingala. Still, she returned to me again and again. Without appointments. She was battling repeated attempts from the government to deport her, the shameless racism of the hostile environment. A monster of a different kind but a monster, nonetheless. When Marie dropped in, she would look for me and sit close to me, often in silence. One evening toward the end of the working day, she came in and started sobbing uncontrollably. Possibly the most sorrowful tears I have borne witness to. She was back. She was not with me, although her body was in the room. I imagined she was reliving massacres. Scenes of war and unspeakable violence. Blood scenes. Scenes of horrors and of loss. It turned out it was the anniversary of the bloody murder of her young son. I sat by her in silence. For perhaps thirty minutes. But I was losing her. She was going deeper and deeper into sorrow. What word of comfort could I even think of giving this horribly traumatized woman who was mourning so painfully the death of her son? How could I reconnect her to the world of the living? Hold her without holding her? And tell her that life was still worth living in the midst of the anti-Black detention she found herself in. Captive, once more, which was compounding her trauma. I stood up, I went to my computer and searched YouTube. I looked for a few Congolese songs and played them. I watched her instantly stand up and start dancing. I joined her. And little by little I could see her rejoining me. Her eyes were alive again. She had returned into the room. Music had brought her back from the dead. And connected us to life.

Engaging with African music took us to a different realm of communication. My intervention with Marie was unusual and intuitive, but our shared Congolese ancestry probably meant I understood perhaps unconsciously the centrality of dancing and music culturally. Current psychological models have not engaged with the worldview and cultural beliefs and values of people of African descent. In fact, they continue to inferiorize them. What is more, the overfocus on the mind and the cognitive has historically marginalized the body. This is at odds with much research that shows the importance of body work and movement in healing trauma. Integrating traditional healing practices into psychotherapy with African and Caribbean clients may address some of the mental health concerns of Black groups.

There are a few noted exceptions related to the exclusion of the body in therapeutic space. **Dance movement psychotherapy (DMP)** is one. In DMP, therapists and clients use body movement and dance to foster the integration and processing of various parts of the self.[8]

DMP is consistent with African and Caribbean healing traditions as an approach. Furthermore, the American Therapy Association now recommends harnessing the power of African Caribbean dance healing systems to process trauma and work with damages done by systems of oppression. According to DMP therapist Maria "Mara" Rivera, that approach, dance and movement, can allow us to reclaim various kinds of powers:

1. **The self-body power**
   The self-body power is about dancing with intention. The intention is to activate healing energy, free intuition, and trust internal resources to do the reparative work. It enables the body to occupy itself.

2. **Collective power**
   Dance has the power to create community connection via the communal spaces it creates. The collective power comes from these spaces, acting as safe container and as a community holding environment for a collective expression, voice, and sharing. Traditionally fostering intergenerational connection and the passing on of healing, culture, and folklore.

3. **Sociopolitical power**
   Dancing and power cannot be separated in Black history. It was through dancing that enslaved Africans connected to the spiritual and found the strength to survive and courage to fight for their freedom. Today dancing and music continue to be central to struggles against oppression and injustice and the reclaiming of power.

4. **Spiritual power**
   African and Caribbean dancing has fed our soul since time im-
   memorial. The energy it generates has the potential to connect
   us to the forces of the universe, to the forces of life, which may
   lead to a subjective sense of oneness and spiritual alignment.

Resisting hierarchies of Blackness

Hierarchies of Blackness have historically been related to proximity to
the master or proximity to whiteness and have therefore relied on colorism. Colorism is the preferential treatment of lighter-skinned people
over dark-skinned ones. Historically, children of Black slaves fathered
by white masters often gained privileges based on their lighter skin
shade, selected to work in the master's house while Blacks of darker
hues were routinely sent to the fields where labor was more intensive
and treacherous. In the African colonies similar systems were created
by colonial powers. In Rwanda, for example, colonial administra-
tors exacerbated divisions by only allowing Tutsis, presumed to be
light-skinned, to attain higher education and hold positions of power
over the dark-skinned Hutus, fueling tensions that significantly contributed to the genocide of 1994.

Colorism has enabled Black people to further their education and
other life opportunities and has encouraged darker-skinned people to
devalue their skin color or seek to lighten it.[9] Over time, class and
status distinctions between lighter- and darker-skinned were created
in the Americas and Africa, with distinction in skin tone mapping directly onto socioeconomic, cultural, and political power and privileges.
This is what is commonly referred to as pigmentocracy.[10]

Pigmentocracy reproduces white supremacy. Another facet of proximity to whiteness is the hierarchization of Black lives based on geopolitical location or, more accurately, proximity to Africa. The trend
across African descendants is to still view Black people in continental
Africa as less sophisticated and more "primitive," in line with colonial fantasies. This leads many people across the diaspora to disown

ancestral ties and Africanness and to see the plight of siblings in Africa as distinct or separate from our experience in Europe or in the US. This is a fallacy.

White supremacy starts with the most expendable lives, which tend to be in the Global South. But it does not stop there. It never has. And so the impunity that protects European states from accountability when it comes to the drowning of Black refugees in the Mediterranean—Black lives attempting to seek safety and security from conflicts often orchestrated to sustain neocolonial interests—creates the type of extreme trauma we saw in Marie. It is the same impunity that ensures that state-sanctioned violence and brutality against Black bodies is allowed to go unpunished in Britain, the US, and in other parts of the West. And the disregard for Black African lives simply feeds into the contempt toward Black bodies everywhere on the planet.

Colonialism and capitalist exploitation of Africa has resulted in catastrophic, irrevocable damage to our planet and led to the global inequalities that threaten peace and harmony in the world. So-called discussions about "development" therefore fit within a wider discussion about environmental damage, racial injustice, and racial trauma. Marie's trauma reminds us of the trauma of millions located in or fleeing exploited nations and bears close resemblance to the colonial violence that marked the consciousness and the unconscious of such nations. It is no coincidence, for example, that countries with the most brutal colonial histories continue to suffer the most brutal conflicts today. That wherever rape and sexual abuse were used as mass weapons of colonial subjugation, where mutilation and unspeakable torture were normalized, we continue to see them today used as weapons of war. Remember, nations can suffer trauma too. And, again, trauma tends to repeat itself.

When we see our fates and suffering as interconnected, we resist "divide and rule" and hierarchies of Blackness that fundamentally reproduce white supremacy. Reclaiming the most devalued, the most disenfranchised, and the darkest and poorest among us is a powerful demonstration of self-love. It is resisting whiteness and all deriving hierarchies.

Beauty as resistance

In "And Still I Rise," Maya Angelou powerfully articulates her capacity to connect with her beauty and her erotic power.[11] Qualities that, despite violent erasure attempts, remain. She evokes the misogyny and racism, contemporarily and historically, that she and generations of Black women before her have endured. Yet her poem is one of triumph, one of survival. Not only have we survived, we are thriving and gaining strength, beauty, and power not despite but because of racial adversity. Though this may challenge common wisdom around the hierarchization and posited pyramids of human needs, there is a long history of marginalized people seeking affirmation through beauty. Black artists and others, for example, have used fashion and style as means to resist oppression for centuries. From the slaves who took pride in their appearance and beauty by dressing in their Sunday best, to the dandies of the Harlem Renaissance and the *sapeurs* of the Congo.[12]

These efforts were never simply about vanity, narcissism, or emulating the master. They have always been about politics, about challenging colonial narratives about self-love and self-definition. We know that connection with beauty during war has been a way to assert one's humanity. An activist recounted the story of such a woman who had spoken about how important it was for her to die beautiful and that if she was to be killed by a sniper, she wanted her killer to know that he was putting a beautiful woman to death. Few domains exist where marginalized women can feel valued and take control of how they are represented. The subordination of our needs is socially expected, and, as part of that, self-negation and self-hatred are viewed as standard. Wearing lipstick during a war had become a way for some to assert their humanity.

The scholar bell hooks teaches us that self-love is dangerous and threatening in a white supremacist culture. She says it is a "serious breach in the fabric of the social order."[13] Reclaiming beauty. Ours. That exists in the world, through art and through nature. Doing so has always been central to liberation.[14] It buffers the impact of racial injustices. At its most fundamental, caring about the way we look is caring about our body and, by extension, our life. It is rejecting notions of inferiority and inadequacy. It is proclaiming, "I believe I am entitled to love and thus to justice and equality." It is quietly saying, "I am a human being. Like you." Perhaps this is what so many have a hard time accepting.

Black mediocrity, Black liberation?

It is hard to write about self-care in the middle of global anti-Black warfare. But there is a war too that is happening inside of us. Many of us try to manage it by overachieving. As I write, the idea that for us to be accepted as human we must become superhuman is still a thing. We must be the next Muhammad Ali of our field. Mediocrity is not an option, it is forbidden to us, therefore being mediocre is not something we dare to allow ourselves to be. Society tells us that to deserve to live, we must have some rare and incredible talent. In art, in sport, in science. In any field, if we are exceptional enough, then people might forgive and forget our Blackness. We might transcend our race, they say. An expression that filled Ali's obituaries, by the way. His greatest achievement was this, it appears. Forget his radical politics. His boxing excellence. Or his sense of justice and ethics. He made white people forget his race. Not when they sent him to jail, mind you. Still, we hear, he made white people connect with him, so many of them tell us, despite his Blackness.

Black excellence is linked to this idea of transcendence.[15] Fundamentally it is the idea that exceptional achievements by Black people, often despite racial adversity, elevate Blackness and counter racist stereotypes about us. Black excellence is, of course, exclusionary and arguably reproduces materialistic takes on what success looks like. It fundamentally centers whiteness as the kid to impress. The internalization of racism can often mean that we are raised and socialized to prove that we are good enough to be recognized and seen. This posturing fuels the belief that any "failure" or mediocrity might confirm racial stereotypes or bring shame onto our family or our community.[16] It also shows little consideration to the impact on our health, physical and mental. I find myself remembering conversations I had with a teacher who had been promoted to deputy head in her school and started working eighty hours a week, every week, until she became so unwell that she had to be hospitalized. Or the Black taxi driver who worked nights and went to university during the day. He suffered the same fate. Both became psychiatric patients. Arguably lucky to be alive.

I have heard of others who did not survive the pressure of Black excellence. When thinking about Black excellence, we must think about how it may be an act of compensation for structural racism but also an act of compensation for shame. Black excellence, insidiously, by parading achievements by Black people, to prove our competence, our capability, and ultimately our humanity, reproduces white supremacy and Black shame. The shame we are talking about here comes about as a result of trying to fit into white society, which consistently tells us implicitly or explicitly that we are inferior, threatening, or otherwise dysfunctional and that we must assimilate into whiteness to be human, alienating us from parts of ourselves that many of us then come to despise.[17] In other words, race-related shame is a by-product of power structures and of racialized social hierarchies. The shame is linked to survival, so it may exist even when we may not have consciously bought into our own inferiority. The awareness that we must "play the game" to survive may bring it up. It is thus a shame that may also be triggered by the contemplation of our complicity. Thankfully, this is something all of us can become aware of and reduce.

Black pride

When your dignity is repeatedly hit and you witness or experience humiliation and indignity, your sense of pride can fundamentally shift. Although pride is the antidote to shame, it requires work. It is difficult to feel pride when you are not represented, when the history that is sold to the world positions you as inferior. When the harm that was done to you and your ancestors under the guise of "civilization" continues to be presented as virtuous. All Black movements for liberation have centered the need for Black pride again, as an act of active defiance. Black pride in this context is a response to white supremacist cultures and ideologies of devaluation, denigration, and Othering. It encourages us to celebrate our heritage, our features, and history. It makes us feel good about being Black. Racism assaults our self-esteem, pride helps maintains it.[18] This is important as research shows that self-esteem may help buffer racist experiences and racial trauma. More frequent experiences of racism are associated with lower self-esteem. And higher levels of self-esteem are associated with lower levels of racial trauma. Clearly, as Black people, our sense of self-esteem is also connected to our racial identity and thus to race. Racial identity concerns a person's self-categorization and attachment to both their racial group and their relationship with whiteness. And, again, research shows that those whose racial identity centers on conformity to whiteness, on devaluing attitudes toward Blackness, and on disconnection from or dissonance with their Blackness are also more psychologically vulnerable within white supremacy.

Acculturation offers us another framework with which to look at our relation to our racial identity. Broadly speaking, as applied to individuals, acculturation refers to changes that take place as a result of contact between two different cultural groups.[19] Acculturation is most often studied in individuals living in countries or regions other than where they were born, thus among immigrants, refugees, asylum seekers, and sojourners. And while it goes without saying that Blackness in the context of Britain or Europe does not imply migration, a large proportion of Black people in the UK or in Europe either have parents or grandparents who were migrants. However, in the US, as previously discussed, the foreign-born population is growing. Given the large cultural differences that exist between mainstream white America and Black American values, worldview, and culture, we may argue that a similar process may need to happen for Black Americans to connect with racial identity development (see chapter 1). As such, the framework is still helpful to think about identity. Acculturation considers migrants' responses to migration and the shifts that occur to their racial and cultural identity because of migration. Acculturation is generally used to consider migrants' responses to migration and the shifts that occur to their racial and cultural identity because of migration. However, the framework is equally applicable to the shifts that might occur when dissimilar cultures come into contact within the same nation. So, the framework offers important insights to help us understand some of the processes that might become engaged when Black Americans interact with the dominant white culture. The model is based on two axes of culture acquisition, which is about how we manage the "new culture" and heritage retention.

These two dimensions intersect to create four possible acculturation styles:

- Assimilation: when we adopt the dominant culture and discard the culture of our heritage.
- Separation: when we reject the dominant culture and retain the heritage culture.
- Integration: when we both adopt the dominant culture and retain the heritage culture.
- Marginalization: rejection of both the heritage and culture of our heritage.

There is now substantial evidence that suggests that discarding our culture of origin or heritage increases the likelihood of a whole host of negative physical and mental health consequences. Generally, those who manage to maintain some contact with their heritage fare much better than those who do not. It is clear, then, that maintaining Black pride is more than a political imperative—it must be central to our self-care.

Resistance through spirituality

Spirituality does not have to be tied to any religion, although, for many of us, religion allows us to connect with the spiritual. Religion and Blackness have a complex relationship. Both Islam and Christianity were imposed on our ancestors. The imperative to forgive has historically been weaponized, as illustrated by the words of Kenyan prime minister Jomo Kenyatta: "When the Missionaries arrived, the Africans had the land and the Missionaries had the Bible. They taught how to pray with our eyes closed. When we opened them, they had the land, and we had the Bible."[20] Christianity's love and mercy messages were sold to our ancestors during the arduous Middle Passage, on torturous plantations, and on native and African shores during colonial encounters between white and Black bodies.

There is absolutely no doubt that a version of Christianity was instrumental in advancing imperial and colonial agendas. White agendas. Christianity was used to justify enslavement. To pacify distraught and furious displaced and tortured bodies and souls by offering them the promise of eternal life. It promulgated a vision of a white god as the image of the white colonial master, and it forever traded forgiveness for mass atrocities and inescapable racial violence. Yet enslaved people did use religion to resist and to survive slavery and to reclaim their humanity. Further, African traditions were combined with Christianity, allowing for a new collective identity and pride to be born.[21]

Today young Black people are shying away from and leaving organized religious institutions, to connect with African and nature-centered spirituality.[22] Reverence for spirits and the ancestors through the practice of Vodou, Santería, Candomblé, or other variations of Yoruba religious traditions is becoming a way to reconnect to one's ancestry while integrating African religious traditions.

Mainstream mental health services are becoming more open to the integration of spiritual practices within mental health care. In the UK, the Royal College of Psychiatrists reported that patients who engage in spiritual practice of some kind gained:

- better self-control, self-esteem, and an increase in confidence
- faster and easier recovery (often through healthy grieving of losses and through recognizing their strengths)
- better relationships with themselves, others, and God/creation/nature
- a new sense of hope and peace of mind, enabling them to accept and live with continuing problems or to make changes where possible[23]

There is therefore a strong case for rediscovering or discovering some form of spiritual practice to heal from racial trauma.

BLACK JOY

The late Toni Morrison wrote about the mystery of the tree-shaped scar, the beautiful scar left on the back of whipped slaves that eerily resembles a tree. It is, for me, a visual representation of her work and life mission. A reminder of the importance of finding joy and beauty within ourselves and within this brutal world. Beauty and joy amid the dehumanizing and violent reality of white supremacy. Joy amid pain. Powerful aspirations in their simplicity. Powerful also in their humanity. Something that reminds me of the genius of Morrison. Her mastery of the art of making the complex and sophisticated not only accessible but so viscerally beautiful. We struggle in "our" culture to celebrate and to mourn at the same time but living while Black is recurrently having to experience anger and pain. The tree-shaped scar is a powerful reminder that beauty can be found in the ugliest of circumstances. And a reminder that life coexists with death, beauty with pain, and that growth can take place in the midst of suffering.

Many come to see me because they struggle with finding joy. Finding joy in intimate relationships. Finding joy in connection. Finding joy in sex. Finding joy just existing in the world while Black. When you cannot find joy for long enough, despair can come knocking, and it is easy to let it in. As we saw in chapter 2, rates of mental health problems and psychological distress are the highest in Black groups. And again, psychological distress is the antithesis of joy. There are less obvious reasons why many struggle with experiencing joy. We may stop ourselves from experiencing happiness or engage in self-destructiveness out of loyalty for those who have suffered or indeed been destroyed. We may feel compelled to experience feelings that were too dangerous to express or experience by those who came before us. Mourning on their behalf. We may stop ourselves from experiencing joy out of fear that we may be punished or that something terrible may be on its way. We may stop ourselves from connecting with joy because we feel, consciously or otherwise, that we simply do not serve joy. Practicing joy must be strategic, and it must be deliberate and like self-care more generally cannot be decontextualized. The ability to create and hold spaces for our joy as individuals and as a group of people is an ongoing struggle. But experiencing joy, even if moments of it, is revolutionary. Joy is a spiritual practice. It connects us to beauty, to wonder, to grace, to pleasure. It is thus an emotion that connects us to life, to the universe, and to ourselves and each other. Black joy disturbs whiteness because it is humanizing, and, because it is humanizing, it is transgressive. White supremacy has been founded on the enactment of sadism, and sadism is all about deriving pleasure, often sexual, through inflicting pain, humiliation, and discomfort. White sadism is therefore all about depriving us of joy. And so, if sadism is central to the reproduction of racist violence, then experiencing joy is central to Black liberation.[24]

TRIPLE CONSCIOUSNESS

I read a lot and follow some people on Twitter, I educate myself, I try to educate myself on these issues and so I'm aware of like things that suggest unconscious bias, microaggressions, macroaggressions. [. . .] I've also read a couple of books, for example, Why I'm No Longer Talking to White People About Race *and, like, the author was able to articulate a lot of the things I was feeling.*

The quote is from a Black male in his early forties who I interviewed as part of my research on racial trauma. In the quote, he shares experience of what he had found helpful in coping with the impact of racism. It reflects the experience of other participants in the study as well as my clinical experience outside the study.

In *The Souls of Black Folk*, W. E. B Du Bois defines his concept of double consciousness, the internal twoness that is necessary for Black people to adopt as they walk through the world, inhabiting two sets of consciousness because of racism.[25] Experiencing the world through the eyes of their oppressor and thus their devaluation of Blackness but also with the adoption of ways of being in the world and our consciousness and its own associated worldview and experience. In order to resist racial trauma and to keep our sanity, I suggest that we need to develop an additional level of consciousness, a level above the primary and secondary levels, which allows us to see conflicts, make sense of them, and remember that power is at play.

In my research, participants were empowered by speaking about their experience. Emerging from the silence was central to the participants' healing journeys. This process relied on having the language, frameworks, and conceptual tools to formulate one's experience and thus regain a sense of epistemic confidence. This triple-consciousness is required to develop a critical approach to reality and to understand the operationalization of power and thus see structures of power that underscore the need for **conscientization**. Conscientization is the process of becoming a critical thinker and unpacking dominant and oppressive thoughts that result from the cycle of socialization.[26]

LEARNING YOUR POWER

The accessibility of psychological concepts, frameworks, and tools has been greatly facilitated by social media and helps bridge intergenerational conversations. Many of us who now have children have committed to breaking the silence on racial injustice and to the articulation of previously unutterable experiences, transmitting tools to self-affirm and challenge the implicit dominance or hegemony of whiteness. Gaining power is a process of conscientization, which is to become conscious of the political, socioeconomic, and cultural oppressive forces underpinning our experience and to gain the confidence to resist them.

There is a tendency to consider power as an all-or-nothing game and to put the psychological burden of atrocities and injustice on Black people. We need to challenge this notion and focus on the losses, the trauma-related effects of white violence on white people. Consequences of racial trauma for white groups, although beyond our remit, need considering, too, and not only because they are central to the reproduction of whiteness but also because focusing on whiteness as a system born out of pathology helps us reject psychological dysfunction. "White fragility" is a perfect illustration of this psychological vulnerability.

Learned helplessness is a phenomenon that has been observed in both humans and other animals who have endured trauma and mistreatment. When experiencing pain or discomfort, eventually, after enough conditioning, the animal will stop trying to avoid the pain at all. Even if there is an opportunity to truly escape it. The internalization of power relations means that we also come to expect that there is nothing we can do to change our circumstances, and, of course, this serves whiteness. There are real power asymmetries that exist in the world, but power is shiftable; we have seen over and over that we do have the power to make radical change in our life. Also, remember that there are various kinds of power. It is important to hold on to this reality.

SELF-COMPASSION

"Compassion" literally means to co-suffer or to "suffer with."[27] It is defined as the feelings that arise in us when we are confronted with the suffering of others and that trigger an urge to alleviate that suffering. Self-compassion can therefore be understood to mean extending compassion to ourselves when we experience suffering or when we feel inadequate, and taking actions to relieve our suffering. American psychologist Kristin Neff, who based her **formulation** of self-compassion on Buddhist teachings, proposes that self-compassion is composed of three main components: self-kindness, common humanity, and mindfulness. She defines self-kindness as being warm toward ourselves when faced with pain and shortcomings rather than ignoring our feelings or resorting to harsh self-criticism. Common humanity involves recognizing that suffering and feelings of personal failure are part of what makes us human. They are part of a shared human condition. Finally, Neff conceptualizes mindfulness as the act of being balanced toward our emotions and feelings by neither suppressing nor exaggerating them. To Neff, this is about observing with openness and nonjudgmental feelings.

This conceptualization of self-compassion reminds us that "the very definition of being human means that one is mortal, vulnerable and imperfect."[28] Current mainstream thinking around self-compassion is color-blind. I have long been advocating for a more radical use of self-compassion. One that takes our sociopolitical realities into account and similarly centers resistance. We know that individuals who are poorly treated in the world tend to treat themselves poorly. When we live in hostile environments, we tend to be hostile toward ourselves as we learn to resort to using self-criticism and shame to manage psychological distress and pain. One may say, we internalize the hostility of our environments and come to relate to ourselves in the same way the world has treated us.

Similarly, as we have seen with Black excellence, facing feelings of mediocrity may be particularly painful for Black people because of internalized racism. Connecting to fallibility may be seen to amount to accepting racist notions of inferiority. It may increase our sense of vulnerability in the world. Black people as a group may well be the most forgiving and generous group of human beings on this earth. Yet when it comes to how we treat ourselves (and each other) we can be very unkind. Of course, this is another consequence of internalized racism. By treating ourselves harshly when we are experiencing pain, by not attending to our suffering when we feel inadequate, and by silencing these experiences, we disconnect ourselves further from our own humanity, we isolate ourselves. From a more radical sociopolitical perspective, by treating ourselves harshly we essentially do the "master's work": we objectify ourselves and reproduce societal contempt toward Black bodies. Self-compassion helps break the cycle. In doing so, it reengages us with the fullness of our humanity.

Using compassion and self-compassion to relate to each other and ourselves also seems consistent with more Afrocentric worldviews. Striking similarities between the Buddhist conceptualizations of self-compassion and Ubuntu philosophy can be made. "Ubuntu" is a Zulu term that describes the essence of being human: "Muntu" = "a human being"; "Ntu" = "human." "Umuntu Ngumuntu Ngabantu" is generally taken to mean we are people because of other people; in other words, we can only exist through other people. And it is the humanity of others that gives us our humanity and vice versa. Being is therefore a process by which we become aware of the us in others and the others in us. Ubuntu places emphasis on the interconnected nature of human experiences or how our internal worlds are inseparable.[29] This African philosophy rests on the belief that every person and every life comes into being through social consciousness, mutuality, and connection. Applying Ubuntu in the context of healing and wellness means seeking to actualize these existential and spiritual dimensions as we navigate white supremacy.

SUMMARY

1.

There is a long Black history of resistance that has historically been erased, pathologized, or interpreted through the lens of self-protecting white supremacy.

2.

Anti-Blackness assaults our dignity repeatedly and cumulatively. This can lead to racial trauma and experiences of humiliation but can be mitigated by cultivating Black pride, connecting with beauty and with joy.

3.

Reframing Black excellence and instead aiming to show ourselves kindness and self-compassion can be freeing for Black groups, and, as part of that, reclaiming our right to be mediocre is reclaiming our unconditional humanity.

4.

Learning to theorize our experience is central to trusting our reality and to making sense of the world. The trusting and naming of our experience is a way to regain a sense of power and agency in the world.

RACE REFLECTIONS

Resisting racism and healing from racial trauma entails our active participation. Resisting is not a passive game. And, similarly, in a context of white supremacy, we simply cannot realistically hope to be well, stay well, and thrive without dedicating some effort. This section gives you the opportunity to reflect on resistance and healing to help ensure you have what you need to thrive.

The last part of the book consolidates our learning process and invites you to commit to a self-care routine.

What have you found most troubling in this chapter?

You may want to explore your bodily responses, images, and thoughts that came to you and explore what they might take you back to. Please use the Race Reflections reflective model (p. 183) to help you.

_____

_____

_____

_____

_____

There are so many ways to resist, and there is no magic formula to survive and thrive within white supremacy. And often those who enact racist violence are also more likely to proclaim what Black resistance should look like.

Thinking about your worldview and white supremacy, what are your expectations of Black people? What do you tend to do when those around you behave in ways that challenge your sense of what resistance should look like?

_____

_____

_____

_____

_____

Black resistance has an exceptionally long history of condemnation, pathologization and shaming, which naturally serves the status quo.

Thinking about your own resistance, what actions have led to condemnation, pathologization, and shaming? What has that taught you about white supremacy? How have you changed or adapted as a result?

_____

_____

_____

_____

_____

Racism robs us of the essence of our humanity. It often leaves us unable to enjoy the beauty that exists in the world. It distracts us from what feeds the soul and connects us to the world.

Take time to consider what additional opportunities you may create to pay enough attention to beauty in all its manifestations. Art, fashion, nature … there is beauty all around us if we pay attention. Taking in as much of it as we can is a way to connect to the universe and to find meaning in the world.

_____

_____

_____

_____

_____

ACTION POINT

CHART YOUR RESISTANCE HISTORY

We discussed how we internalize societal contempt and shaming, including messages of dysfunction and pathology in relation to Black resistance, even though we know what the function of these messages is. Remember, we are socialized to serve the needs and maintain the comfort of those with more power, and we will therefore likely frequently experience discomfort, tension, or an internal conflict when we resist.

In order to externalize or challenge the centering of whiteness within ourselves, it is helpful to remember how much we as a people owe to the resistance of our parents, forebears, and ancestors.

Your action point: Find out what your resistance history looks like. You may find looking at the history of resistance from those around you, including your parents, inspiring. Similarly, please do some research to be more familiar with how freedom fighters have consistently been ill-treated within white supremacy and how, over time, they have come to be defined as heroes.

THRIVING WHILE BLACK

Navigating the world while Black can seem like being in a maze. There is no doubt that white supremacy inflicts harm and that this harm is often invisibilized. Racial trauma, as we have seen, is complex. It operates at many levels and often affects several generations, who become engaged in repeating histories, unaware that they are fulfilling scripts the world needs them to fulfill.

We have seen that trauma can leave us vulnerable to experiencing helplessness and to believing that we are powerless. In fact, society and white supremacy have much vested interest in us believing that we are.

We are not powerless. And Black lives do matter. Our stories matter.

Powerful Black people have always been feared. Especially when they draw from ancestral wisdom and memory and their hunger for justice and for freedom.

The world depends on us internalizing powerlessness, and so we may come to fear our own power and thus fear ourselves.

This fear of power is something each of us must confront. And like most of the experiences in the book, it does not sit in isolation from sociohistorical contexts. But the fear of our own power and the transformational potential it offers can stand in the way of our liberation, of us centering our needs and acting in a way that sustains us and resists racism.

This is the reason so many of us deny ourselves our creativity and why so many of us leave our gifts unwrapped. We make the decision—conscious or otherwise—not to materialize our potential because of this deep-seated fear.

But we sit at crossroads many times in our lives.

Perhaps even many moments in the day. The direction we take at these junctions is up to us. I hope *Living While Black* has provided enough material, tools, and reflections to help some of us to take a different direction or at least to be mindful of our steps. We do have the power to make different choices even as we remain constrained within the violent structures of anti-Blackness.

The freedom to choose direction is power. Where do we go from here? The familiar road? The one that guarantees a degree of safety because of familiarity . . . or do we choose the unknown? Do we take the way of uncertainty, trusting the path laid by our ancestors? Trusting our intuition and our body?

We deserve to be free. And we deserve to thrive. It is time to connect with our power.

YOUR RADICAL
SELF-CARE PLAN

Self-care has been co-opted and misused. It has become synonymous with consumerist images of white women pampering themselves, sanitizing its radical origins. The politics of self-care finds its origin within the racial struggle, and it became a central part of movements for justice, liberation, and equality. Although the radical origins of self-care lie firmly in the civil rights movement, it was women and in particular Black feminist scholars who made it an integral part of their praxis, as evidenced by the following Audre Lorde quote, possibly the most well-known quote on self-care: "Caring for myself is not self-indulgence, it is self-preservation, and that is an act of political warfare."

To Lorde, self-care is an act of defiance. Indeed, when systems are designed to harm you, if not kill you, and you insist on staying alive and well, you are challenging the very fabric of society and the social order. The quote from Lorde is extracted from *A Burst of Light*, a book she wrote shortly after being diagnosed for the second time with cancer. This personal context adds poignancy and depth to her political call. Her life was under assault from patriarchy, homophobia, and racism. Her life was in peril not only from these systems but also from cancer. The threat of death was real, and so was the yearning for loud and powerful survival. So loud it still resonates.

Lorde's self-care call was also a call for self-love at a time when Black bodies were despised and subjected to overt hateful violence.

In this context, self-love is also about Black love. Self-care is love for Black people. Practicing self-care within a white patriarchal society screamed Black Lives Matter well before we started saying Black Lives Matter. Audre Lorde thus reconnects us with the intended direction of self-care. Self-preservation. And, specifically, self-preservation as political warfare. Today things are arguably different, but the struggle for racial justice is ongoing in the United States, in the UK, in France, and in most Western nations. It may look different, but it is the same struggle in the Global South.

As I write, Black people are, it feels, under constant assault. Social media means images of dead Black bodies are constantly doing the rounds in front of our eyes. Drowning en masse in the Mediterranean because of anti-Black border control. As well as dying disproportionately of COVID-19. Since we witnessed the video of the suffocation of George Floyd, protests are ongoing and racial inequalities are recurrently making headlines as topics of conversation. Rarely ever, though, as topics of action. And, in the midst of this normalized violence, we are invited to "debate" our humanity and welfare again and again.

Most of us aspire to be the best version of ourselves and to at the very least survive. But we need to be bold and aspire to do more. To thrive and to be well. Practicing self-care is essential to buffer the impact of racism and racial trauma on us, which is a prerequisite to living a good life while Black. The present plan has been designed to encourage and support these efforts. It aims to encourage you to reflect and to set goals or aspirations in relation to your welfare and psychological development as a Black person.

The plan is focused on your body, mind, and soul, and their interconnection. It also seeks to help you connect to who you are as a whole and connect to the world around you to ultimately support your growth. You are invited to engage with the suggested activities regularly—ideally, if you can, use the journal from your first action point. Frequencies are suggested. Please feel free to vary them; for example, increase usage during times of stress.

1: NURTURE YOUR BODY (DAILY)

Our body is our primary tool of resistance. As we have seen throughout this book, racism has deleterious effects on both our body and our mind. We as a community can be rather neglectful of our physical health. We therefore neglect our main tool of resistance, our main boundary, our main refuge.

Although this relative cultural neglect of our physical health must be located within a context of structural racism, intergenerational trauma, and internalized racism, many of us need to relearn our relationship with our bodies and start to show both gratitude and appreciation for them keeping us alive and functioning in the midst of racial violence. A negative attitude toward our bodies encourages us to neglect, abuse, and harm ourselves and reproduces societal contempt toward Blackness.

This may require a shift in our attitude and treatment of ourselves, including the value we place on our body. The start of this growth plan invites you to reflect on possible devalued stories you may have internalized about your body. They may be related to Eurocentric standards of beauty and racial stereotypes, or they may be in response to repeated experiences of denigration. In this section you are invited to relate to your body with kindness, gratitude, and love. You may want to use this space to address your body and write loving words to it directly (e.g., "You have continued to help me despite …") or pay special attention to specific body parts you want to start to engage with in a more loving way. Some people find expressly asking their body forgiveness helpful.

NURTURE YOUR BODY

2: DO A "JOY INVENTORY" (WEEKLY)

Black joy is the ultimate tool of defiance. It can also be the most difficult practice to engage in and to sustain within white supremacy and thus in the midst of Black pain. There are various reasons society finds Black joy intolerable, but part of the reason is that it humanizes us. It renders us complex and multidimensional beings capable of the full range of emotions.

Experiencing joy and pleasurable activities acts as a strong buffer against hopelessness and low mood. In psychological jargon this is referred to as "behavior activation." Please take some time to write down all the things that bring joy and commit to doing them regularly. Commitment without a plan, however, is like traveling without a passport. It reduces the chances of us getting far.

Therefore, in a second part of this activity, plan pleasurable activities you have identified in your list. What is planned is much more likely to get done. Make sure you do a little bit of that joyful stuff every day. Set alarms on your phone, write them in the journal, and make time to do them. This is also part of reprogramming our relationship with our body and recalibrating our brains.

JOY INVENTORY

3: CHECK YOUR ACHIEVEMENTS (MONTHLY)

When we experience racism, it is easy to forget what we have achieved and become consumed with self-doubt, feelings of inadequacy, and/or feelings of powerlessness. The reality is that, as we go through difficult experiences, we also learn key skills and strategies to navigate the society that has been handed to us. Make time to remember victories big and small. This will help increase your sense of agency and mastery but also remind you to learn from your experience.

Please complete a record of your greatest achievements. They can be little things or large things. Things you do for yourself and things you do for others, professional or community-related activities. You may want to ask two or three people you trust. It would be helpful if at least one of these people is not related to you. Ask them to list your greatest achievements as they see them. Compare the information you obtained to the achievements you came up with. Add any information missing. Reflect on any discrepancy; many of us tend to minimize our achievements. Regularly revisit this list and add achievements as they arise.

ACHIEVEMENTS

4: DO A QUALITY INVENTORY (MONTHLY)

Once you have completed your achievement checklist, it will be much easier for you to see your gifts, talents, and the aptitudes you possess. Many of us find it difficult to tolerate our giftedness. But it is important that we learn to take this in. In a racist society, it is natural and understandable to internalize racist fantasies or stereotypes that are projected onto us and to define ourselves in a way that is consistent with others' prejudices and expectations. Over time some of us may lose sight of what we're good at.

As with the previous activity, make a list, but this time of what you're good at. There should be at least seven gifts, talents, or aptitudes.

Make it a habit to revisit this list, too, particularly when you are going into spaces where you are underrepresented or before an important evaluation. Doing a quality inventory can be a helpful way to reconnect ourselves to all that we have to offer to the world and to build our self-esteem. A higher self-esteem has been found to mitigate the negative impact of racist violence. Maintaining a healthy self-esteem is therefore important work to engage in.

INVENTORY

5: CONNECT WITH BLACK PRIDE (MONTHLY)

What is it about being Black that you love, if not adore? Despite racism, few of us would swap racial background given the choice. This tells us that we know that Blackness entails beauty and gifts and that there are plenty of things we would not change about living while Black. What makes you feel grateful for being Black? What about Blackness brings you a sense of pride? When do you most feel proud about being Black? Let us try to document those things for *you*.

It is important that you define for yourself what brings you pride; this may be quite different from those around you, and that is okay. This is not about agreement or consensus. This is about your personal connection or affiliation with Blackness. About your personal relationship with Blackness and how you experience and perceive it.

CONNECT WITH BLACK PRIDE

6: MAP YOUR LINEAGE

Try to locate yourself in terms of family lineage as far back as you can go. Find out as much as possible about your relatives on both sides of your family; if possible, do a family tree. As you do, you may also want to think about the skills and traits people have in common and those you share with others. What relationships are strong? Which are weak? Where does trauma lie? Some of us who by reason of adoption, estrangement, or other separation cannot complete this task about our biological families may want to use our chosen or adopted families to do this. In this case it may be helpful to consider and rank closeness on three levels using circles.

Draw a circle and put yourself in it. People you add in that first circle would be those you are closest to. Outside this circle, draw a second circle and put in it people in your chosen family who matter to your welfare but whom you feel less close to. In the final circle, put the names of those who are members of your chosen or adopted family but who you feel the least connected to. Think about traits, attributes, personality, and life experiences that people have in common in these three circles and those you share or may not share. Map anything that may be relevant, such as interests, professions, and personality, and relate this material to you. See the patterns that emerge in this physical representation of your home. Once your circle is completed, please revisit it two to three times a year; update it as appropriate. I suggest you place it in a private area you can easily access.

MAP YOUR LINEAGE

7: LEARN ABOUT BLACK HISTORY (ALL YEAR)

The framework of Black history remains a controversial one. There is no history that is uniquely Black, and what we construct as Black history is often recounted through a white European gaze. Nonetheless, here we use the expression to refer to historically significant events and processes when it comes to our identity and worldview. As Black people, so many of our events and stories have been deformed and twisted to maintain the illusion of white supremacy. There is so much about Black history we do not know about because of systematic erasure and revisionism. Finding out more through our own research and reading is a lifelong journey. And it is a journey of self-discovery too. However, it is important that we see Blackness as being located within specific sociohistorical and economic contexts and remember those most likely to have been disappeared under the same hierarchies of power and proximity to the white European master.

Ask yourself: What would I like to know more about? What knowledge have I been deprived of? If I were writing a history book, what chapter might I first want to write? What do I need to know about history to better understand my lived experience today?

This section invites you to make a discovery plan and a research plan about Black history. The above questions will guide your research and help you set priorities.

BLACK HISTORY

_____

_____

_____

_____

_____

8: FOSTER BELONGING (MONTHLY)

Cultural homelessness is said to occur when we feel neither quite at home within the culture of our parents or heritage nor in that of the country we were born or reside in. Often, this is due to repeated experiences of marginalization, discrimination, or Othering. It is the sense of not feeling quite at home anywhere. Cultural homelessness can leave us feeling vulnerable, unprotected, and forever in search of belonging. This cultural alienation and yearning are central to the experiences of many Black people. And it could most definitely be a manifestation of racial trauma.

There are various ways to increase our sense of belonging. Affirmations can work for some; for example, "I belong," "I have as much right to be here as others," or "My forebears built this country." For others, it may be helpful to remember that experiences of cultural homelessness are a function of our social location more than they are a reflection of our actual right of abode. People with more social power usually struggle much less with entitlement in relation to space and land, irrespective of how illegitimate their claims might be. Use this space to note the things (or people) that remind you that you belong. Revisit and add to this monthly.

FOSTER BELONGING

_____

_____

_____

_____

_____

9: CONNECT TO YOUR HERITAGE

We know that having a positive relationship with our ancestry and heritage often acts as a buffer when it comes to experiences of racism. It can truly help provide protection to ourselves and increase our sense of homeness. It is thus so important that we feel a sense of connection to Blackness and/or African-ness as well as, where possible, the culture and heritage of our parents, grand-parents, and/or forebears.

What do you know about this aspect of your identity and heritage, the way of thinking, the way of feeling, the food, the music, the communities, and so on. What can it teach you about the world? About resistance, about love, about harmony, about spirituality? Seeking to better understand various aspects of this heritage will help develop your sense of connection to it.

You are entitled to reclaim these cultural ties and develop a sense of ownership. However, as you engage or reengage with your cultural heritage, please use a critical lens, and remember that we are socialized to assess non-Western cultures via a Eurocentric and white normative thought. Whenever possible check your findings with relevant communities.

CONNECT TO YOUR HERITAGE

_____

_____

_____

_____

_____

10: CONNECT WITH NATURE (WEEKLY)

Most non-Western worldviews have historically held connection with nature as central to wellness and social harmony. This is the case for traditional African beliefs too. Although these beliefs have long been belittled in Eurocentric and white normative thought, plenty of research is now documenting how connecting with nature fosters human flourishing and enhances our social, psychological, and relational life. Exploring or experiencing nature, living near nature, or even viewing nature have all been shown to have positive effects on our minds, bodies, and social interactions. What is even more encouraging is that nature can help us process trauma and increase our well-being. Therefore, reclaiming nature is important to our resistance and self-care as Black people. Our ancestors are part of nature. They are in the air we breathe, the ground we walk on. They are all around us and in us.

There are several ways we can get closer to nature, even those of us stuck in urban jungles and with concrete and cement as landscape. Here are a few suggestions: Can you visit a green space regularly? If not, can you grow something? Even if this is only on your windowsill and in a tiny pot? Nurturing a plant and growing a seed is one of the cheapest ways to connect with nature and greenery. Failing all these, you may have to use the power of your imagination by making efforts to visualize natural landscapes such as forests, parks, or beaches and making it a habit to create a green corner in your mind. Nature-based relaxation aids can be easily found online, or you may simply wish to obtain paintings, pictures, or photographs of nature.

CONNECT WITH NATURE

_____

_____

_____

_____

_____

11: MAKE INTERGENERATIONAL LINKS (MONTHLY)

If this is possible for you, consider strengthening connections with the land(s) of your heritage and ancestry. Remember there are many among us within our communities who act as bridges between our ancestry and the present and may hold some of this history. Do you have conversations with the elders in your family and/or community? Seek to connect with them regularly; they are a rich source of experience and invaluable living archives that we tend not to use. Seek connection in their experiences. Hear and record their stories. Nature may also be used here to forge these ancestral connections. Here is a possible activity to mindfully connect with our ancestors through nature: Stand barefoot on grass or soil. As you do, focus on the connection between you and the earth. Take in all the sensation that you can grasp through your senses. The color, the smell, how the meeting of your being and the earth feel.

Now visualize communities that came before you and walked that very same earth, smelled the very same grass, and stared at the same soil. We share these elements. Nature is also a mechanism of connection with the past. By deeply connecting with earth and nature's elements we are also connecting with our ancestors. If you have the possibility of going to the land(s) of your heritage or ancestry, bring back a little soil if you can. The act of feeling and smelling that soil when you are away can connect you to your history and ancestry.

MAKE INTERGENERATIONAL LINKS

12: FEED YOUR SOUL (WEEKLY)

We are a highly musical people. We have used music through the centuries to share stories, pass on heritage, build community, and fight racial oppression. It is this extraordinarily rich and complex history that is revealed through the way we move our bodies to music and the way our soul becomes enlivened through rhythms. Music is a deeply spiritual practice that allows us to reach a different experiential field. We can facilitate this process by using drumming.

Drumming has long been used to promote healing and the expression and processing of grief and trauma throughout the Global South and in Africa. It has been used for millennia to improve physical, mental, and spiritual health. Again, we have increased evidence that drumming, particularly when done in community, alleviates trauma-related distress. Engaging in drumming therefore fulfills a varied purpose. It may connect us to our spiritual self, connect us to the motherland, and help heal trauma. If drumming is not possible, consider joining a community dance group, ideally a form of dance that directly connects you to your heritage (the choice is vast).

FEED YOUR SOUL

13: NURTURE YOUR COMMUNITY (WEEKLY)

Whiteness, as we have seen, has eroded our community and ancestral ties. Our personal healing cannot be separated from the healing of our community. We are so interdependent that we cannot exist or do well if we have no community or if our community is hurting. This is the spirit of the African philosophy of Ubuntu. We are because you are. Our fate and our wellness cannot be separated. Looking after our community is looking after ourselves too.

Furthermore, one of the most important things you need to think about is how you are going to sustain yourself. None of us can do this self-care alone, at least not effectively. Social support is incredibly important to survive racism. Vital, even. Not only will it act as an additional buffer, but we do know that Living While Black leaves us vulnerable to chronic exclusion, ostracization, and, for many of us, further marginalization. Of course, risks are not equally distributed. Your positionality and the social power this affords you can reduce or increase the above risks. Nonetheless, these risks exist for everyone. Nurturing your community is nurturing yourself.

NURTURE YOUR COMMUNITY

14: GET ORGANIZED (MONTHLY)

Pursuing anti-racism and any kind of liberation requires becoming fully aware of oppressive systems and their impact on individuals and on groups. But anti-racism is more than an intellectual pursuit. Some say it is a verb. It is a "doing." Engaging in activities aimed at dismantling white supremacy and all systems of oppression takes critical reflection and action. This is what is commonly referred to as "praxis." Social organizing fulfills various goals. It brings people together and creates a sense of community and togetherness around shared concerns. It shares and collectivizes the responsibility for social change. It helps us connect, see one another, and thus humanize us all. It allows us to regain a sense of power and keep the bigger picture—the structural picture—in mind.

There are various ways to work toward social change, and there are various ways to do social organizing. For this activity, get familiar with groups and communities working toward racial justice or equality that are in operation at the grassroots level in your locality. Connect with them. Try to have conversations with at least one of them. Think about ways you may be able to support them or contribute to their efforts, but also get support from them.

GET ORGANIZED

PSYCHOLOGICAL TOOLS

RACE REFLECTIONS REFLECTIVE MODEL

Reflectivity may be taken as the process of learning from our experience to grow, develop, and gain new insights into ourselves, others, and the world. Several reflective practice models exist. Few, if any, pay attention to embodied data, yet as we engage in reflection it is important to remember the body, given the potentially triggering impact of race-based material. The Race Reflections reflective model supports a holistic engagement with knowledge and data.

Each time you are exposed to new information, particularly information that challenges your worldview, pause to engage in the reflective cycle on the next page. This will help you process information more deeply and engage with your body, cognitively as well as emotionally.

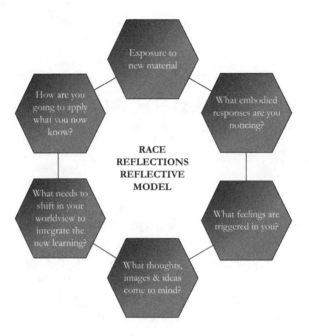

RACE REFLECTIONS INTERSECTING IDENTITY STAR

The Race Reflections Intersecting Identity Star is a tool designed to encourage reflections on positionality. "Positionality" refers to where we stand within social structures and the impact of the various axes of oppression that shape our social identities and worldview as well as access to power. These axes include (but are not limited to) race, class, gender, gender expression, sexual orientation, religion, and ability status, as well as all their intersections.

The point of this tool is to help you visualize some of the most common social identities and their intersections, reflect on both privileged and marginalized identities, and approach racial trauma and racism in a way that is nuanced and considers the multiple identities we all occupy.

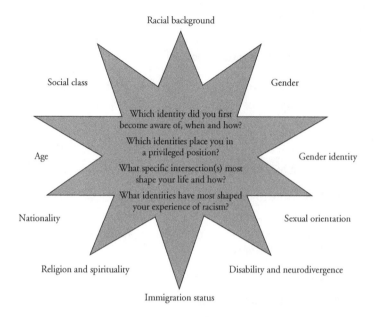

Racial background

Social class

Gender

Which identity did you first
become aware of, when and how?

Which identities place you in
a privileged position?

Age

Gender identity

What specific intersection(s) most
shape your life and how?

What identities have most shaped
your experience of racism?

Nationality

Sexual orientation

Religion and spirituality

Disability and neurodivergence

Immigration status

VISUALIZING SAFETY

Feeling unsafe in the world is associated with trauma, and while we can never feel completely safe in white supremacy, nor would it be adaptive, feeling constantly alert to possible dangers is not only exhausting but can also deeply affect our physical and psychological health. However difficult it might be, we need to learn to switch off and find safety whenever we can.

Learning to practice relaxation is a fundamental skill to mitigate the stress of racism.

There are various scripts that exist online for the purpose of relaxation. You are free to use them and play around with them and shift them in a way that allows you to make them your own.

Initial instructions

1. Find a place that is safe and quiet and where you expect not to be interrupted.

2. In that space, make yourself as comfortable as you can. You may adopt any position. Choose one that does not make you feel self-conscious or strain your body.

3. Close your eyes, if you feel safe enough to do so. If you do not feel safe enough, lower your head and gaze.

4. Take a few deep breaths. It helps to pay close attention to the air entering and leaving your body and to your tummy (rather than your chest) rising and falling.

Script

You are about to travel to a place of safety, and these directions will help you get there.

The first thing we need to do is find an image or place of safety. It may be real or imagined. It may be a place you have always wanted to go or a place you have visited. Many find visualizing a beach, a forest, or a familiar room helpful, but it could be anywhere.

When you have this place in mind, visualize yourself entering it calmly and noting instantly the relaxing effect that being in this place of peace has on your whole being.

As you start to connect with safety, take a few more deep breaths, and with each breath allow your body to take in the safety and peace all around you.

In order to help your body, take in as much safety as you can. You now want to focus on all your senses. It does not matter where you start. You may want to first concentrate on the sound you hear in this place of safety. What does safety sound like? Pay careful attention.

Once you have spent enough time imagining the sound and hearing it in your mind, you may focus on the colors. What does safety look like? Pay careful attention.

Once you have spent enough time taking in colors in your place of safety, you may focus on the sensations on your skin, the texture, the warmth, and anything you can perceive through your sense of touch.

Once you have spent some time taking in the sensations on your skin, you may want to focus on smell and even taste.

Use at least three different sensory modalities to help your body connect to safety, and experience each for five to ten minutes.

Once you feel relaxed, take a few more deep breaths, and prepare to exit your place of peace and safety, remembering that you carry this place within you and that you can return to it whenever you want or need.

Open your eyes.

Tips

Remember that it is often more helpful to practice visualization and relaxation regularly so that it becomes habitual and more easily called on when needed.

There is really no right or wrong way to practice this script. You may initially struggle to remain focused and find that your mind starts to wander places you do not want to go to.

If that is the case, simply refocus your attention onto your breath, then gently reinvite your mind to one of your senses.

You may initially struggle to do five to ten minutes or to use all sensory modalities, and that is perfectly fine. With practice, you will most likely get there.

Visualization is not for everyone, although I rarely meet people who find it unhelpful.

THE GLASS OF DIRTY WATER

We have seen that racial trauma can cause us to experience high levels of shame. We have also seen that shame serves various functions in society and that it is a by-product of white supremacy.

I use the "glass of dirty water" exercise in therapy. Many patients find it helpful when reconsidering their relationship with shame and in locating it within sociopolitical contexts.

You are invited to get a full glass of water and simply place it somewhere in your field of vision, ideally at eye level. Imagine the water is dirty.

In therapy, I use questions such as these: When was the glass of dirty water first handed to you? How full was the glass? How much of it did you drink? What did the water do to you? How much of it are you still drinking today? Who has been handing you the glasses? Who tends to be handed glasses of shame socially? In situations of abuse of power, who hands who the glass? What makes people more likely to drink the water and why might that be so?

The choice of the word "handed" here is purposeful. It aims to establish a boundary or distance between shame and us as people who experience it. It aims, too, to highlight the possibility of agency, since something that is handed to us symbolically can be handed back or refused. Finally, it reflects that while shame can so easily be taken in, it can similarly easily be shared.

Specific examples may be discussed to highlight the role of racialized and gendered hierarchies in the distribution of shame. So I might ask, in situations of gendered violence (against women), who tends to be handed the glass? Or again, when it comes to economic exploitation, who drinks the water (in colonial situations, etc.)? And, knowing what we know, how might we respond to being handed the glass? Who does the water belong to?

Many people find that water has a grounding effect, and perhaps, too, it helps to bring the sociopolitical into the room in a way that is visual and reversible. If you feel up to it, intentionally pour the water down the drain simply to symbolize you resisting shame that does not belong to you. Feel free to repeat this activity each time you struggle with race-based shame.

THE P.O.W.E.R. FRAMEWORK

As we have seen, trauma deeply affects our physiology and renders us more likely to be reactive or triggered in situations where we feel discriminated against. The P.O.W.E.R. framework exists to manage physiological response and increase our sense of agency and confidence. P.O.W.E.R. stands for Prepare, Observe, Wait, Exhale, and Resist.

Prepare: When it comes to navigating challenging and possibly hostile spaces, preparation is key. Preparation gives us the chance to anticipate and rehearse possible difficulties, challenges, and struggles. These rehearsals increase our sense of readiness and thus confidence, which in turn is likely to increase our agility. Preparation might include anticipating tricky interactions, unwelcome comments, and/or microaggressions and visualizing or rehearsing responses.

Observe: An important skill for us to try to master is the art of observing. Here you are invited to observe what is going on in your body, how you are physiologically responding to the space. Next, pay attention to what is going on at interaction level (e.g., body language, spoken language, space, and airtime taken). Then elevate your observations by identifying power in relation to position-ality but also in relation to the local context (e.g., organi-zational seniority). Once you have a clear sense of where power lies, pay close attention to how it is manifesting in the interaction between people and in relation to you. You may start to observe scripts, patterns, games. Observing is fundamental to understanding what is going on and therefore theorizing about our lived experience.

Wait: Our tendency to react when we see or experience injustice can be explained physiologically. And while there are plenty of situations when reacting will be appropriate and helpful, in many situations, reacting may deprive us of time to strategize. Think about what the safest or most effective way may be to respond or resolve a problem, and simply increase your behavioral choices. For many of us, waiting will allow us to consider all options available.

Exhale: The invitation to exhale (and, of course, inhale) is a reminder to actively and deliberately work on relax-ation in order to help reduce possible anxiety symptoms.

Re-centering our body via our breath is a helpful way to bring our physiology back to baseline, not only to minimize flight-or-fight responses, which increase the likelihood of reactiveness, but also to help ensure the optimal environment for our cognitive abilities. It helps ensure that we can reason, plan, concentrate, and strategize as effectively as possible.

Resist: At this stage you will be in a much stronger position to resist safely and effectively. A reminder: resistance takes various forms. Sometimes you may decide that silence is the best course of action, having taken all circumstances into consideration. Sometimes you will decide that silence is not an option, and you will challenge or confront what was said or done straight away. Alternatively, you may decide that you need more time to seek support and organize. What matters here is that you have consciously thought about what the most suitable course of action may be rather than simply reacted because you were triggered in the moment.

FORMULATING RACIAL DYNAMICS IN GROUPS

This framework uses **group analytic** ideas to help you make sense of race-based difficulties you may come across in institutional settings and in the workplace.

1. What is the problem?

Often, acts of racial bullying or marginalization act as cover for some anxiety-provoking but unnamed problem or disturbance. Revisit the story of Julie as an illustration (p. 71). Your first question is, What is the real problem?

2. **Who is involved and present, and who is involved
   but not present?**
   Linked to the previous question, when we experience
   racial trauma or racist violence, we may come to believe
   that we are the problem or that it is we who need to
   change to make ourselves acceptable. It is important
   to reframe issues of ownership so as not to internalize
   the scapegoat role. Remind yourself that this is a *group*
   problem and that the entire group is involved.

3. **What are the payoffs?**
   There will always be gains for some, conscious or otherwise, in cases of group violence, conflict, or dysfunction.
   Sometimes it is the pure gratification of sadistic impulses. Usually, power games are involved. Think about
   what these payoffs may be in your situation.

4. **What histories are being reproduced?**
   When a person of color experiences racism in social
   structures, it is helpful to link their experience to past
   abusive treatment (their own but also those of the
   group they may belong to) so that possible historical
   scripts, including parental traumatic histories, may
   become visible, addressed, and possibly processed.
   Seeing those patterns can help us to move differently,
   to disrupt the script, and to maximize the chances of a
   different outcome.

RESISTING WHITE PROJECTIONS

This tool uses ideas from **psychoanalysis** to help us resist
white projections. Projection is a psychological defense
that entails displacement. With projection we displace
feelings we are not prepared to own onto an external
object or person. Introjection is what can happen when

we are at the receiving end of "projection." When we introject the projections of others, as we have seen, we identify with them and their fantasies, wishes, and other psychological material. It is a normal process to introject or internalize the psychological world of others—particularly when they hold authority or power in our life. And here lies the problem of internalized racism or the harm in introjecting the racist messages that we swim in.

To build our resistance to racism and racial trauma we need to build stronger psychological boundaries, so that they are less vulnerable (only less, not never) to the internalization of racist violence.

A central tenet of psychoanalysis is that insight is healing and liberating. Insight involves making conscious what may be unconscious and thus naming what may be going on (e.g., what may be projected onto us). This act of externalization can reduce identification with the projected material.

It is likely that such insight will not be sufficient in averting harm in a white supremacist context. However, combined with other interventions, the above psychoanalytic and group analytic formulations can be extremely helpful in buffering the impact of racism on us.

A visualization exercise

Visualizing your skin pores as dilatable and retractable may be a helpful metaphor to represent openness, exposure, and vulnerability to foreign invasion. With this activity, you are invited to connect with your skin, the different sensations you feel, and then to imagine your pores opening when they are safe and closing when they are unsafe or in vulnerable situations. If you prefer, visualizing a flower that can open and close for self-protection can be helpful. Some people find visualizing themselves to be in a protective bubble helpful too. Play around with various metaphors and see what works better for you.

NAVIGATING WHITENESS AT WORK

The whiteness at work formulation is a basic tool anyone experiencing racism at work may use. It is question-based and designed to be simple and accessible. The aims of the tool are to

1. Make sense of oppressive situations by seeing connections, links, and patterns. Formulating and conceptualizing racism/oppression is one of the most powerful methods to retain a sense of agency and power when we experience it.

2. Promote some psychological boundaries and increase our capacity to see the situation in its entirety or from above, thus helping us strategize. Racism is a significant stressor. When we are under stress, our capacity to plan, think clearly, and problem-solve is often significantly impaired. A helicopter view of the situation can help us problem-solve more effectively and stops us from becoming too activated or triggered, therefore reducing the likelihood of psychological injury/trauma.

3. Externalize the problem. Once more, strong structural and psychological factors exist that promote victim-blaming in situations of abuse of power. Further, experiences of racism can quickly hook onto past trauma and abuse and/or psychological "vulnerabilities," increasing their wounding potential. Again, our best defense here is to externalize.

A basic formulation may thus be useful when both navigating and making sense of whiteness at work. The framework is not designed to promote any course of action but aims to encourage reflection and self-care.

Choose your strategies (the framework and basic questions)
This tool may be useful both to those affected by racism and those working to support victims or targets.

1. What is the main narrative/discourse? Ask yourself:
   - What is going on here that sounds typical/predictable?
   - What is causing me distress/discomfort? (Trust your experience.)
   - What seems beyond the individuals concerned?

2. How is whiteness being reproduced here? Ask yourself:
   - What tropes can I recognize?
   - What stereotypes are being used?
   - What structural inequalities are engaged/perpetuated?

3. Who are the agents of whiteness? Ask yourself:
   - Who is actively reproducing whiteness?
   - Who is passively/inadvertently reproducing whiteness?
   - Are there any agents that may be or appear unwilling? (Consider using them in question 5.)

4. What tactics or devices are in use? Ask yourself:
   - What devices are being used to exclude/Other?
   - What is/are the function(s) of those tactics/devices?
   - What is the impact of any tactic used (on me and on others)?

5. Navigational and resistance strategies. Ask yourself:
   - In relation to the function(s) of the devices in use, what strategies are available to me to buffer/counteract?
   - What support is available to me—internally and externally?
   - What/who do I already know that I could summon to help me navigate here?

You may want to organize this information in a table.

Reflect on your answers. Discuss them with others you trust, and, more importantly, derive a plan of action based on what you want to achieve in your current situation and the support you have. Remember, white supremacy is beyond you, and it is beyond me too.

WORKING WITH RACIAL TRAUMA

Blackness-Centered Compassion therapy

In 2017, I developed the Blackness-Centered Compassion model to incorporate the power of self-compassion into our structural realities. The model has at its core the sociopolitical and historical origins of racial trauma, how we cope, and the impact on us trying to survive in a white supremacist culture and all social functions. It also acknowledges the impact of unsafeness or recurrent stressors in the creation of shame and self-criticism as ways of self-relating because, in self-compassion frameworks, the centrality of axes of oppression (e.g., racism in creating feelings of unsafeness) has received little attention.

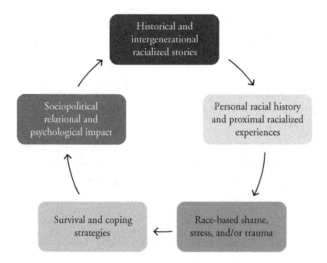

Blackness-Centered Compassion Therapy Formulation (Kinouani, 2018)

The model is a way to make sense of or formulate race-based difficulties.

It links race-based shame and racial trauma to the intergenerational context and to personal histories of resistance and aims to help us understand and explain survival or coping strategies that have been adopted in the context of white supremacy. The point of the model is to foster connection between the "here and now" and the "there and then" in a way that centers the experience of racism.

Historical and intergenerational racialized stories

This covers both historical and family stories related to racism and oppression. They may include how you have been impacted by slavery and colonialism or migration; the experiences of your parents, grandparents, and great-grandparents; or any related story you are aware of that may have shaped your worldview.

Key question to reflect on:

What have you learned about the world, others, and your-self from intergenerational stories?

Personal racial histories and "proximal" experiences (of racism)

It would be impossible to remember every single instance of racism we have experienced. We will likely all have sto-ries that have felt more significant and formative.

Key question to reflect on:

What have you learned about the world, others, and your-self from these experiences?

Race-based shame or racial trauma

This section of the model invites you to reflect on possible trauma and/or shame. We have seen that shame is central to trauma experiences but that it is a difficult emotion to own, even though this shame is largely projected onto us. You may find it helpful to revisit the table of signs and manifestations in chapter 2.

Key question to reflect on:

What has been the impact of these experiences on how you view and relate to yourself and Black people?

Survival and coping strategies

Taking all that we have been exposed to and the mes-sages this might have given us about the world, we know that, as all living organisms do, we have adapted to our environment to survive, although adaptation may look different in different people based on what they have learned about survival. For example, if I have learned that I must work twice as hard to avoid racism, workaholism may be my coping strategy. If I have learned that African features are less valued and should make me feel ashamed, I may seek to attempt to "Europeanize" my appearance.

Key question to reflect on:
What have been my survival and coping strategies?

Sociopolitical, relational, and psychological impact
Of course, any survival or coping strategies we adopt will have consequences. Some will be desired, and some will be unwanted. For example, if I distance myself from my Blackness to survive, this may compound my sense of inferiority or shame, reproduce whiteness sociopolitically, and impact my relationships. I may attempt to avoid close relationships with Black people, or I may be critical of those who choose to connect with their Blackness in a way that is more Afrocentric.

Key question to reflect on:

What has been the impact of my coping and survival strategies on me psychologically, on my relationships with others, and on white supremacy?

The point of the model is not to tell you how to survive white supremacy. Instead it is to help you contextualize how you operate in society as a result of racism and to reflect on the impact with a view to either showing self-compassion and/or how you may have needed to operate. Then, if you so wish, attempt other ways of resisting.

GLOSSARY

A

adverse childhood experiences
"Adverse childhood experiences" (ACEs) refers to traumatic experiences that happen to us before we reach the age of eighteen. The list of ACEs is varied and includes abuse, neglect, bullying, parental trauma, psychological distress, and racism. ACEs are of interest to clinicians and public health professionals because they can often predict health outcomes and statuses in later life.

African American Vernacular English (AAVE)
Also referred to as African American English (AAE) or Ebonics, this is a form of English spoken by Black Americans in the US. It is believed to have connections with languages spoken elsewhere in the Black diaspora (e.g., Jamaica) and in Nigeria.

amygdala
The amygdala is the almond-shaped structure located at the base of the brain, one part in each hemisphere. The amygdala is often referred to as the fear center because one of its primary functions is to activate the fight-or-flight response and modulate the emotional response to threatening stimuli or information.

anti-Blackness
Anti-Blackness is first and foremost antagonism, hatred, or contempt for people racialized as Black because they are Black. Anti-Blackness is structural, psychological, and relational. Anti-Blackness is premised on

the alleged "primitivity" and inferiority of people of African descent and manifests in normalized violence in all domains of functioning for Black people, including legally, economically, and politically. Anti-Blackness is not only a Black and white binary affair. Non-Black groups equally benefit from anti-Blackness and commonly participate in it.

anti-racism

Anti-racism is fundamentally any action we deliberately take to dismantle white supremacy. Anti-racism has been defined as the active and deliberate process of identifying and dismantling racism in all its manifestations so that power may be redistributed and shared equitably in society.

anxiety

Anxiety refers to the condition of being uncomfortable—physiologically or psychologically distressed—because of worry. When persistent or interfering with everyday life, feelings of anxiety may require support or signal "mental health problems."

assimilation

Assimilation in the context of immigration or cultural exchanges refers to the process of taking in full the dominant culture, worldview, and values at the expense of the culture, worldview, or values of one's heritage, ancestry, or marginalized group.

attachment

Attachment refers to the deep and enduring emotional bond between two people characterized by closeness and feelings of security when in the presence of the attachment figure and distress or angst when separated. The first relationship between infant and caregiver is the basis of attachment theory, which sees this relationship as central to an individual's subsequent social, emotional, and cognitive development and ability to form stable relationships with others.

autonomic nervous system

The autonomic nervous system is the part of the nervous system that controls and regulates involuntary physiological processes such as our heart rate, blood pressure, and sexual arousal.

B

Black excellence
Black excellence speaks to the social process by which the extraordinary achievements of Black people are celebrated and promoted by fellow Black people. It is often believed to uplift Black people and/or disrupt stereotypical expectations. Black excellence has gained much traction on social media, where it continues to be supported via the use of hashtags like #blackexcellence.

Black mental health
Black mental health simply refers to the mental health and related issues of those who are racialized as Black.

C

cisgendered heterosexual (cishet)
Cishet is the abbreviation of cisgender (born in the gender one identifies with) and heterosexual (someone typically attracted to individuals of the opposite sex).

colonialism
Colonialism concerns the use of force (often military), violence, or other forms of power by a nation to set up colonies or settlements outside its borders with the aim of increasing its power, influence, and/or resources politically, ideologically, and/or economically.

compassion-focused therapy (CFT)
Compassion-focused therapy is a form of psychological therapy that harnesses the use of self-compassion to reduce psychological distress linked to self-criticalness and excess shame. It was developed by clinical psychologist Paul Gilbert in the late 1990s and early 2000s and has been subject of many studies, which have evidenced its effectiveness within a range of "mental health problems."

conscientization
A term, also *conscienciser*, coined in Frantz Fanon's *Black Skin, White Masks* that describes the development of a critical consciousness that

increases an individual's awareness of unjust circumstances, events, and relations that have become normalized in daily life by consciously adopting an alternative view of oneself and the world.

cultural homelessness

"Cultural homelessness" describes the anxiety of not having a cultural home or belonging to any culture. It is commonly experienced among bicultural or multicultural individuals such as migrants, their children, or those of mixed ancestry. The term was coined by psychologist Veronica Navarrete Vivero in the late 1990s and has since generated much interest.

D

dance movement psychotherapy (DMP)

Dance movement psychotherapy is a form of expressive therapy that uses movement in the form of traditional dances or more subtle forms of movement like yoga and stretching to calm the body and to unlock feelings and emotions trapped within, aiming to help individuals reclaim a connection between actions, words, and emotions.

defense mechanism

A psychological strategy that is used unconsciously to protect a person from anxiety arising from unacceptable thoughts or feelings or parts of the world or ourselves that are too painful or threatening to our sense of self.

les déracinés

A French expression that literally translates as "the uprooted." It is often used as a metaphor to describe immigrants, their children, or those who are seen to be removed from their own cultural setting.

double consciousness

Refers to the internal conflict experienced by marginalized, colonized groups in an oppressive society. First used by Du Bois in *The Souls of Black Folk* to describe the psychological challenge Black Americans face looking at themselves through the eyes of white, racist society.

double jeopardy law (UK)
A piece of legislation that provided that an individual could not be prosecuted for the same crime twice. The law was changed in 2005 as part of Sir William Macpherson's recommendations from the inquiry into the Stephen Lawrence murder case.

drug-induced psychosis
A form of "psychosis" believed to be induced by drugs.

dualism
Dualism refers to the philosophical separation of the body and the mind that has long been attributed to French philosopher René Descartes.

E

embodied/embodiment
We speak of "embodiment" to describe the connection between emotions and the body, the physical manifestation of feelings through bodily sensations, and the way our bodies respond to oppressive sociopolitical realities.

epigenetics
Epigenetics is the study of how our behaviors and environment can change our genes or, more precisely, how genes are expressed.

epistemic homelessness
Epistemic homelessness is the process in which racially marginalized individuals feel disconnected from their sense of truth, of knowing when their experiences of racism are denied by racially privileged individuals. It is the sense of losing one's truth base or anchor as a direct result of the denial of racism. The framework was developed by psychologist Guilaine Kinouani, the author.

F

formulation
Psychologists and especially those who are clinicians speak about formulation when they attempt to make sense of people's presenting difficulties,

complaints, and problems. Most formulations make connections between the past and the present to better understand what might keep patterns going.

G

gaslighting
Refers to a kind of emotional abuse in which the perpetrator seeks to gain power over the victim by making them doubt their thoughts, memories, or feelings.

geopolitical
Related to geopolitics or the influence of power in the world order, in state-to-state or international relations. The term "geopolitics" was coined by the Swedish political scientist Rudolf Kjellén in the early twentieth century.

goal-striving stress
"Goal-striving stress" names the theory that covers the discrepancy between our aspiration for and achievement of a better way of life, weighted by the subjective probability of success, and the level of disappointment experienced if those life goals are not realized, particularly for people of color who have to battle for equality, status, and position in social structures that exclude them.

group analysis
Group analysis is both a method of understanding processes and dynamics in groups, including social groups, and a clinical method to support people who have experienced psychological distress. Group analysis seeks to consider individuals in their family, historical, and cultural contexts, and uses networks of communication as the basis for treatment and intervention.

H

hippocampus
The hippocampus is the part of the brain located in the inner (medial) region of the temporal lobe of the brain. It is implicated in various func-

tions, including memory formation, orientation in time and space, and the regulation of emotional responses.

homeness
"Homeness" here refers to the feeling of homeliness, being connected to a place that feels like home.

I

imperialism
Imperialism concerns the use of force (often military), violence, or other forms of power by a nation to influence, control, or take over other nations, usually with the aim of territorial expansion and/or increasing the imperial nation's power, influence, and/or resources politically, ideologically, and/or economically.

imposterism (imposter syndrome)
"Imposterism," or "imposter syndrome," refers to subjective feelings of fraudulence or to the fear of being "found out" that is experienced by high-achieving marginalized individuals in work settings. The framework was developed in the 1970s by psychologists Pauline Clance and Suzanne Imes, who reasoned that gender norms, sexism, and discrimination led to highly capable women feeling like imposters at work. Further research has since established that the phenomenon exists along other axes of oppression.

inflammation
Inflammation is the body's defense against things that harm it, such as infections, injuries, and toxins. When something damages our cells, our body releases chemicals (e.g., cortisol) that trigger a response from the immune system to help us. Stress has been shown to interfere with our body's inflammatory responses.

intergenerational trauma
Trauma that is transferred between generations. First recognized in children of Holocaust survivors but widely documented in descendants of slaves, Native Americans, war survivors, refugees, and survivors of interpersonal abuse.

intersectionality
A term coined by Kimberlé Crenshaw as a way of analyzing the social world to make visible the particular ways axes of oppression, such as race, gender, social class, and so on do not exist in isolation but shape one another and create particular experiences and forms of structural vulnerabilities.

J

John Henryism
A way of coping with racism and racist discrimination by working extra hard to succeed. Sustaining such levels of effort results in a range of negative physiological consequences in Black American populations, including hypertension. The term was coined by Black American epidemiologist Sherman James in reference to the nineteenth-century Black American railroad worker John Henry, who died of physical exertion.

M

medical model
The term "medical model," from psychiatrist R. D. Laing, refers to the "set of procedures in which all doctors are trained." It includes complaint, history, physical examination, ancillary tests if needed, diagnosis, treatment, and prognosis with and without treatment. When we think about the medical model in relation to mental health, we mean a perspective or set of ideas that center the medical origin and management of mental health problems.

medium secure unit
Psychiatric inpatient treatment facility providing care for adults with complex mental health problems who have been in contact with the criminal justice system and who may present a severe risk to themselves or others. Research has consistently found that Black groups in the UK are much more likely than any other to be treated in medium secure units.

mental health

There is no universally agreed definition of mental health, and how we define it will say much about our worldview and philosophical beliefs. Many define mental health as the absence of mental health problems, seeing wellness through the prism of the psychiatric classification system or the medical model. Many disagree. Generally, though, it is helpful to think about mental health as our ability to lead fulfilling lives and feel connected to the world and people around us.

Mental Health Act (1983)

The Mental Health Act is a piece of British legislation that covers the compulsory treatment and detention of people diagnosed with psychiatric disorders that may put themselves or others at risk. Being detained under the Mental Health Act is sometimes called being "sectioned," in reference to the different sections of the act.

mental health problems

Again, since there is no universally agreed definition of mental health, how we define mental health problems is similarly variable. If we see mental health through the prism of psychiatric classification systems, those meeting criteria for diagnoses such as depression, anxiety, or schizophrenia would be deemed to have mental health problems. It is important to remember the criticisms in relation to the Western and individualistic bias in this belief system and understand that there are other ways to think about psychological distress or disturbance (for example, by considering white supremacy as psychological pathology).

microaggressions

A term coined by African American psychiatrist Chester Pierce to describe the commonplace daily verbal, behavioral, or environmental indignities, whether intentional or unintentional, that communicate hostile, derogatory, or harmful racial slights and insults toward people of color.

misogynoir

"Misogynoir" is the combination of two terms: "misogyny" (hatred of women) and "noir" (the French word for black). "Misogynoir" therefore describes the anti-Black misogyny that Black women experience. It genders anti-Blackness or racializes misogyny targeted at Black women specifically. The term was coined by Black feminist scholar Moya Bailey in the late 2000s.

N

neocolonialism
Popularized by Ghana's first president, Kwame Nkrumah, in the early 1960s, "neocolonialism" refers to the intrusive (mis)management and continuity of the former colonizer's power through economic, political, and educational systems.

neuroplasticity
"Neuroplasticity" (or "neuronal plasticity") refers to the brain's ability to adapt and create new connections between our neurons. We rewire our brains to adapt to new circumstances.

neuroscience
The scientific study of the nervous system, which aims to help us understand how the brain works and its fundamental properties.

O

ontological insecurity
When an event or experience challenges or threatens feelings of safety and security within one's own life or existence.

P

Pan-Africanist (Pan-Africanism)
Pan-Africanism is a philosophical belief system and a cultural and political movement that seeks Black liberation through unity, solidarity, and connection of people of African descent throughout the world.

patriarchy
A social system and way of organizing the world that ensures the continuing dominance, privileges, and power of those who are men or those

deemed "masculine" and the marginalization and oppression of women or those deemed "feminine." Patriarchy, like all systems of oppression, relies on very strict policing of binary gender constructions and on being invisible from those who benefit the most from it.

place attachment
An emotional bond to place/space, which may be a sense of familiarity, belonging, or rootedness in a place defined by cultural history or heritage. The source of "place attachment" is attributed to social environment psychologists Irwin Altman and Setha Low.

postcolonialism
This term is taken to refer to world order after widespread independence from Western colonialism, the various ways colonialism shaped the world order, and the movement that seeks to reclaim and rethink the history and agency of people subordinated under colonialism.

Post-Traumatic Slave Syndrome (PTSS)
A framework created by author Joy DeGruy that highlights the survival strategies adopted by Black American communities and other members of the African diaspora to survive chattel slavery and other related racial trauma that are transferred through the generations and remain in operation today.

post-traumatic stress disorder (PTSD)
A condition that can develop after an individual has witnessed or been involved in a traumatic event (or events). The condition was first recognized in war veterans and has been known by a variety of names, such as "shell shock." But it's not only diagnosed in soldiers—a wide range of traumatic experiences can cause PTSD.

prefrontal cortex
This is the part of the brain referred to as the cerebral cortex. The cerebral cortex is the thin layer of the brain that covers its outer part. The prefrontal cortex covers the front of the frontal lobe. Prefrontal cortex functions include our social behaviors as well as our executive functions, such as planning, concentrating, and making decisions.

projection
A psychological defense mechanism conceptualized by Sigmund Freud to describe the process by which unwanted thoughts, motivations, emotions, and impulses are attributed or transferred to another person.

projective identification
A psychological process or defense by which we take in others' projections (e.g., disowned feelings, impulses, fantasies) as though they were ours and behave, feel, or think in accordance with them. Projective identification is one of the more complex defense mechanisms, with a full theory going back to British psychoanalyst Melanie Klein's work on infant functioning.

prone position
The position is that of an individual lying face-down, with their chest on the ground. The prone position when used in restraint is particularly dangerous and has been linked to high risk of death by asphyxia.

psychoanalysis
Various theories and clinical and social approaches related to the study and theorization of the unconscious and the treatment of psychological distress. Psychoanalysis is premised on the existence of an unconscious, a psychic or psychological reservoir of those parts of us or the world we lack awareness of but that affect our relational and communicational arrangements.

Psychological formulation
Psychologists and especially those who are clinicians speak about formulation when they attempt to make sense of people's presenting difficulties, complaints, and problems. Most formulations make connections between the past and the present to better understand what might keep patterns going.

R

racial identity development
We speak of racial identity development to speak of the process by which we grow in our sense of affiliation, belonging, or identification with a racial group.

respectability politics
An expression used to refer to the politics of those who are from marginalized groups and who advocate assimilation, decorum, and the acceptance and mimicking of dominant values. In the context of race, it means embracing white middle-class ways of being and thinking to bring honor and "be respectable" to in an attempt to overcome racism.

S

schizophrenia
Schizophrenia is categorized as a "severe and enduring" psychiatric condition with a vast array of symptoms, chiefly unusual perceptions or beliefs that are inconsistent with those held in one's sociocultural group, such as seeing or hearing things others don't or believing things others struggle to understand. Schizophrenia belongs to the family of psychoses. Psychoses are mental states characterized by losing touch with reality.

severe and enduring mental health problems
Describes diagnoses of mental health conditions that are expected or believed to affect a person throughout their lifetime. In the UK they include diagnoses of bipolar disorder and schizophrenia. They are often opposed to "common mental health problems," which are believed to carry less risk and be more easily manageable and treatable and include issues such as depression and anxiety.

social construction
Social construct(ion)s describes things or concepts that have no "objective" or "real" existence except what we as a society and by consensus have decided.

social inclusion
The practice to ensure that various groups of people can take part in society fully and can tackle social structures, policies, or processes that exclude disadvantaged groups.

stereotype
An overgeneralized belief about a particular class or group of people, regardless of its individuals' behavior.

structural racism

"Structural racism" refers to the racism that is embedded in social structures such as schools, the police, and/or the military. This form of racism is often hidden and not consciously enacted. It exists because these structures were configured to serve the interests of white groups and as a result disadvantage people of color through procedures, processes, and practices that discriminate against people of color at a collective level.

structural violence

A term coined by Norwegian sociologist Johan Galtung that refers to social structures and economic, political, medical, and legal systems that perpetuate inequity through the unequal distribution of power and disproportionately affect marginalized groups and communities.

T

The Talk

"The Talk" refers to the conversation parents have with young Black children to prepare them for racism and in particular the dangers of encounters with the police and other authority figures, with a view to increase their chances of surviving these potentially deadly exchanges.

telomeres

Sections of DNA found at the ends of each of our chromosomes; they help to protect the ends of our chromosomes from damage or fusing with nearby chromosomes. With age or stress, telomeres have been shown to shorten.

U

unconscious bias

Also known as implicit bias, unconscious bias refers to the underlying attitudes, prejudices, and stereotypes we hold toward people who evade our conscious awareness but still influence the behavior and treatment of these groups.

W

whiteness

Whiteness is a social system that ensures the production and reproduction of the dominance and privileges of people racialized as white.

whitening the race (racial whitening)

Racial whitening is an ideology centered around the idea that Black inferiority or "the Black problem" could be resolved over successive generations by "breeding" exclusively with white people. It was believed that over time such selective and racially motivated breeding would lead to the genetic, cultural, and social improvement and ultimately the disappearance of the Black race. Although the ideology is more strongly associated with Latin America, it has been found in parts of the Caribbean.

ACKNOWLEDGMENTS

To everyone at Penguin Random House and particularly to Marianne Tatepo, thank you for giving me the opportunity of a lifetime. This book would not have seen the light of day without your vision, guidance, and encouragement. To Maya Fernandez and the team at Beacon Press, thank you for your support and for giving the book a home in the US.

I want to wholeheartedly thank those who have shared words, silences, tears, and laughter with me, particularly research participants of my doctoral thesis, on which *Living While Black* is partly based. Those who have made me feel and think and thus grow as a researcher, as a clinician, and as a human. All your voices and experiences and some of my early writing have led me here, to this book.

To Black Twitter, to which I owe so much of my intellectual growth and sanity, thank you. You have allowed me to keep thinking when my thinking was under attack; you have given me the intellectual community I needed to grow as a scholar.

A few god-sent people joined me on my journey; they have smoothed the road so I could keep walking along the path of academia. Chief among those are Beverley Stobo, Joanna Wilde, Joanna Bennett, and Derek Tuitt. I do not know that I could have kept going or kept hopeful without your support.

Thank you to the whole Race Reflections community, including members, clients, and our first assistant psychologists, Leone Alexander and Charlotte Maxwell, for walking alongside us as we took our first steps as a social enterprise and for your support. Thank you to those who have cast their eyes on early manuscript drafts and provided feedback and encouragement, particularly Martha Crawford, Kate Hammer, and Alex Thomson.

Most importantly, thank you, Maman. For teaching me moral courage, dignity, integrity, resistance, and the value of education.

Finally, to that shy and anxious little Black girl in the banlieue, the hopeless daydreamer who learned about the injustices of this world way too early: You and I know the odds were stacked against us. But we are here. And I am giggling with you. Thank you for fighting all the battles you have had to fight to get us both here.

NOTES

Introduction

1. K. B. O'Reilly, "AMA: Racism Is a Threat to Public Health," *American Medical Association*, November 16, 2020, https://www.ama-assn.org/delivering-care/health-equity/ama-racism-threat-public-health.
2. G. Kinouani, "Reflections on Being a Black Client and a Black Therapist," *Race Reflections*, July 24, 2018, racereflections.co.uk/reflections-on-setting-up-a-private-practice-part-1-the-gap.
3. Michael Omi and Howard Winant, *Racial Formation in the United States: From the 1960s to the 1990s* (New York: Routledge, 1986).
4. M. Ralph and M. Singhal, "Racial Capitalism," *Theory and Society* 48, no. 6 (2019): 851–81.
5. A. Smedley and B. D. Smedley, "Race as Biology Is Fiction, Racism as a Social Problem Is Real: Anthropological and Historical Perspectives on the Social Construction of Race," *American Psychologist* 60, no. 1 (2005): 16–26.
6. Suman Fernando, *Institutional Racism in Psychiatry and Clinical Psychology: Race Matters in Mental Health* (Cham, Switzerland: Palgrave Macmillan, 2017).
7. Calvin Schermerhorn, *The Business of Slavery and the Rise of American Capitalism, 1815–1860* (New Haven, CT: Yale University Press, 2015).
8. Theodore W. Allen, *The Invention of the White Race* (London: Verso, 1994).

Chapter 1—Being Black

1. G. Kinouani, "Racial Trauma, Silence and Meaning," *Race Reflections*, April 20, 2019, racereflections.co.uk/racial-trauma-silence-and-meaning.
2. G. Kinouani, "On School, Institutional Racism and Everyday Violence," *Race Reflections*, June 10, 2019, racereflections.co.uk/on-school-insititutional-racism-&-everyday-violence.

3. R. Hamad, *White Tears/Brown Scars: How White Feminism Betrays Women of Colour* (Melbourne: Catapult, 2019).

4. M. M. Accapadi, "When White Women Cry: How White Women's Tears Oppress Women of Color," *College Student Affairs Journal* 26, no. 2 (2007): 208.

5. G. Kinouani, "Silencing, Power, and Racial Trauma in Groups," *Group Analysis* 53, no. 2 (2020): 145–61.

6. "History Is Repeated in Protests at the Death of George Floyd; Echoes of 1968," *Economist*, June 1, 2020, www.economist.com/united-states/2020/06/01/history-is-repeated-in-protests-at-the-death-of-george-floyd.

7. Y. Steinbuch and J. Fitz-Gibbon, "Worldwide Protests Break Out over George Floyd's Death," *New York Post*, June 3, 2020, nypost.com/2020/06/03/global-protests-break-out-over-george-floyds-death.

8. b. hooks, *All About Love: New Visions* (New York: Perennial, 2001).

Chapter 2—Black Minds

1. Great Britain, Department of Health, *Delivering Race Equality in Mental Health Care: An Action Plan for Reform Inside and Outside Services and the Government's Response to the Independent Inquiry into the Death of David Bennett* (London: Department of Health, 2005).

2. K. Bhui, S. Ullrich, C. Kallis, and J. W. Coid, "Criminal Justice Pathways to Psychiatric Care for Psychosis," *British Journal of Psychiatry* 207, no. 6 (2015): 523–29.

3. J. Y. Nazroo, K. S. Bhui, and J. Rhodes, "Where Next for Understanding Race/Ethnic Inequalities in Severe Mental Illness? Structural, Interpersonal, and Institutional Racism," *Sociology of Health and Illness* 42, no. 2 (2019): 262–76, doi.org/10.1111/1467-9566.13001.

4. J. Das-Munshi, D. Bhugra, and M. J. Crawford, "Ethnic Minority Inequalities in Access to Treatments for Schizophrenia and Schizoaffective Disorders: Findings from a Nationally Representative Cross-Sectional Study," *BMC Medicine* 16, no. 1 (2018): 55.

5. F. Keating, "African and Caribbean Men and Mental Health," *Ethnicity and Inequalities in Health and Social Care* 2, no. 2 (2009): 41–53.

6. C. C. Lo, T. C. Cheng, and R. J. Howell, "Access to and Utilization of Health Services as Pathway to Racial Disparities in Serious Mental Illness," *Community Mental Health Journal* 50, no. 3 (2014): 251–57.

7. S. M. De Luca, J. R. Blosnich, E. A. Hentschel, E. King, and S. Amen, "Mental Health Care Utilization: How Race, Ethnicity and Veteran Status Are Associated with Seeking Help," *Community Mental Health Journal* 52, no. 2 (2016): 174–79.

8. E. Ward and M. Mengesha, "Depression in African American Men: A Review of What We Know and Where We Need to Go from Here," *American Journal of Orthopsychiatry* 83, nos. 2–3 (2013): 386–97, doi:10.1111/ajop.12015.

9. M. A. Gara, S. Minksky, S. M. Silverstein, T. Miskimen, and S. M. Strakowski, "A Naturalistic Study of Racial Disparities in Diagnoses at an Outpatient Behavioral Health Clinic," *Psychiatric Services* 70, no. 2 (2019): 130; S. M. Eack, A. L. Bahorik, C. E. Newhill, H. W. Neighbors, and L. E. Davis, "Interviewer-Perceived Honesty as a Mediator of Racial Disparities in the Diagnosis of Schizophrenia," *Psychiatric Services* 63 (2012): 875–80.

10. R. Schwartz and M. Blankenship. "Racial Disparities in Psychotic Disorder Diagnosis: A Review of Empirical Literature," *World Journal of Psychiatry* 4, no. 4 (2014): 133–40; K. Halvorsrud, J. Nazroo, M. Otis, E. Brown Hajdukova, and K. Bhui, "Ethnic Inequalities in the Incidence of Diagnosis of Severe Mental Illness in England: A Systematic Review and New Meta-Analyses for Non-affective and Affective Psychoses," *Social Psychiatry and Psychiatric Epidemiology* 54 (2019): 1311–23, doi.org/10.1007/s00127-019-01758-y.

11. C. Couto, S. Barreto, and M. L. Rolim Neto, "Suicide in Black Children," *International Journal of Social Psychiatry* 64, no. 5 (2018): 506–8; R. Holliday-Moore, "Alarming Suicide Trends in African American Children: An Urgent Issue," SAMHSA, July 23, 2019, https://blog.samhsa.gov/2019/07/23/alarming-suicide-trends-in-african-american-children-an-urgent-issue.

12. Halvorsrud et al., "Ethnic Inequalities in the Incidence of Diagnosis of Severe Mental Illness in England."

13. J. Tolmac and M. Hodes, "Ethnic Variation among Adolescent Psychiatric In-Patients with Psychotic Disorders," *British Journal of Psychiatry* 184, no. 5 (2004): 428–31.

14. *Independent Inquiry into the Death of David Bennett* (Norfolk, Suffolk, and Cambridgeshire Strategic Health Authority, [2003]), image.guardian.co.uk/sys-files/Society/documents/2004/02/12/Bennett.pdf; R. Norton-Taylor, ed., *The Colour of Justice: Based on the Transcripts of the Stephen Lawrence Inquiry* (London: Oberon Books, 1999).

15. J. Bor, A. S. Venkataramani, D. R. Williams, and A. C. Tsai, "Police Killings and Their Spillover Effects on the Mental Health of Black Americans: A Population-Based, Quasi-Experimental Study," *Lancet* 392, no. 10144 (2018): 302–10.

16. E. Frankham, "Mental Illness Affects Police Fatal Shootings," *Contexts* (American Sociological Association) 17, no. 2 (2018): 70–72, https://journals.sagepub.com/doi/pdf/10.1177/1536504218776970.

17. Suman Fernando, *Institutional Racism in Psychiatry and Clinical Psychology: Race Matters in Mental Health* (Cham, Switzerland: Palgrave Macmillan, 2017).

18. K. Bhui et al., "The Impact of Racism on Mental Health: Briefing Paper," Synergi Collaborative Centre, March 2018, https://synergicollaborativecentre.co.uk.

19. N. G. Harnett, "Neurobiological Consequences of Racial Disparities and Environmental Risks: A Critical Gap in Understanding Psychiatric Disorders," *Neuropsychopharmacology* 45 (2020): 1247–50.

20. S. Karlsen, J. Y. Nazroo, K. McKenzie, K. S. Bhui, and S. Weich, "Racism, Psychosis, and Common Mental Health Disorder Among Ethnic Minority Groups in England," *Psychological Medicine* 35 (2005): 1795–1803; "Trauma," *APA Dictionary of Psychology*, dictionary.apa.org/trauma.

21. American Psychiatric Association, Task Force on DSM-V, *Diagnostic and Statistical Manual of Mental Disorders: DSM-5*, 5th ed. (Washington, DC: American Psychiatric Association, 2013); K. Kirkinis, A. L. Pieterse, C. Martin, A. Agiliga, and A. Brownell, "Racism, Racial Discrimination, and Trauma: A Systematic Review of the Social Science Literature," *Ethnicity and Health* 26, no. 3 (2018): 1–21.

22. R. T. Carter, "Race-Based Traumatic Stress," *Psychiatric Times* 24, no. 14 (December 2006): 37–38, www.psychiatrictimes.com/view/race-based-traumatic-stress.

23. S. P. Harrell, "A Multidimensional Conceptualization of Racism-Related Stress: Implications for the Wellbeing of People of Color," *American Journal of Orthopsychiatry* 70, no. 1 (2000): 42–57.

24. J. C. Alexander et al., *Cultural Trauma and Collective Identity* (Berkeley: University of California Press, 2004).

25. R. P. Knight, "Introjection, Projection, and Identification," *Psychoanalytic Quarterly* 9, no. 3 (1940): 334–41.

26. S. Sullivan, "Inheriting Racist Disparities in Health: Epigenetics and the Transgenerational Effects of White Racism," *Critical Philosophy of Race* 1, no. 2 (2013): 190–218.

27. Z. Avramova, "Transcriptional 'Memory' of a Stress: Transient Chromatin and Memory (Epigenetic) Marks at Stress-Response Genes," *Plant Journal: For Cell and Molecular Biology* 83, no. 1 (2015): 149–59.

28. S. L. Mangassarian, "100 Years of Trauma: The Armenian Genocide and Intergenerational Cultural Trauma," *Journal of Aggression, Maltreatment and Trauma* 25 (2016): 371–81; B. Münyas, "Genocide in the Minds of Cambodian Youth: Transmitting (Hi)stories of Genocide to Second and Third Generations in Cambodia," *Journal of Genocide Research* 10, no. 3 (2008): 413–39.

29. J. Salberg, "When Trauma Tears the Fabric of Attachment: Discussion of 'The Intergenerational Transmission of Holocaust Trauma: A Psychoanalytic Theory Revisited,'" *Psychoanalytic Quarterly* 88, no. 3 (2019): 563–82; M. S. Sharpley, G. Hutchinson, R. M. Murray, and K. McKenzie, "Understanding the Excess of Psychosis among the African-Caribbean Population in England: Review of Current Hypotheses," *British Journal of Psychiatry* 178, no. 40 (2001): s60–s68.

30. B. van der Kolk, *The Body Keeps the Score: Mind, Brain and Body in the Transformation of Trauma* (New York: Penguin, 2015).

31. P. Gilbert, "The Origins and Nature of Compassion Focused Therapy," *British Journal of Clinical Psychology* 53, no. 1 (2014): 6–41.
32. R. Pal and J. Elbers, "Neuroplasticity: The Other Side of the Coin," *Paediatric Neurology* 84 (2018): 3–4.
33. Gilbert, "The Origins and Nature of Compassion Focused Therapy," 6–41.
34. A. Alkozei, R. Smith, and W. D. S. Killgore, "Gratitude and Subjective Wellbeing: A Proposal of Two Causal Frameworks," *Journal of Happiness Studies* 19, no. 5 (2018): 1519–42.

Chapter 3—Black Shame

1. K. W. Crenshaw, "Demarginalizing the Intersection of Race and Sex: A Black Feminist Critique of Anti-Discrimination Doctrine, Feminist Theory, and Anti-Racist Politics," *University of Chicago Legal Forum* 140 (1989): 139–67.
2. L. B. Watson, C. DeBlaere, K. J. Langrehr, D. G. Zelaya, and M. J. Flores, "The Influence of Multiple Oppressions on Women of Color's Experiences with Insidious Trauma," *Journal of Counselling Psychology* 63, no. 6 (2016): 656–67.
3. Frantz Fanon, *Black Skin, White Masks* (London: Paladin, 1970).
4. G. Kinouani, "Internalised Racism and the Colour of Power," Race Reflections, July 18, 2019, racereflections.co.uk/internalised-racism-the-colour-of-power.
5. A. Khan, "Science File: Black Men's Plight as 'Superhuman'; Bias That Minority Males Are Bigger, More Menacing Than White Men May Play Role in Police Shootings," *Los Angeles Times*, March 15, 2017.
6. G. Kinouani, "Shame and Marginalisation: An Intersubjective Formulation Model," Race Reflections, October 18, 2015, racereflections.co.uk/shame-and-marginalisation-an-intersubjective-formulation-model.
7. M. D. Pickersgill, "Debating DSM-5: Diagnosis and the Sociology of Critique," *Journal of Medical Ethics* 40 (2014): 521–25.
8. G. Kinouani, "Culturally Biased CBT, Part 2: Injustice and Depression," Race Reflections, June 1, 2017, racereflections.co.uk/culturally-biased-therapy-part-2-injustice-and-depression.
9. G. Kinouani, "Epistemic Homelessness," Race Reflections, November 1, 2020, racereflections.co.uk/epistemic-homelessness.
10. C. Pierce, "Offensive Mechanisms," in *The Black 70's*, ed. F. Barbour (Boston: Porter Sargent, 1970).
11. John Bowlby, *Attachment and Loss*, vol. 1, *Attachment* (New York: Basic Books, 1969); C. H. Zeanah, L. J. Berlin, and N. W. Boris, "Practitioner Review: Clinical Applications of Attachment Theory and Research for Infants and Young Children," *Journal of Child Psychology and Psychiatry* 52, no. 8 (2011): 819–33.

12. M. C. Hidalgo and B. Hernandez, "Place Attachment: Conceptual and Empirical Questions," *Journal of Environmental Psychology* 21, no. 3 (2001): 273–81.

13. G. Kinouani, "On Home, Places, and Loss," Race Reflections, May 21, 2020, racereflections.co.uk/on-attachment-place-and-otherness.

14. C. Yeo, "Briefing: What Is the Hostile Environment, Where Does It Come From, Who Does It Affect?," Free Movement, May 1, 2018, www.free movement.org.uk/briefing-what-is-the-hostile-environment-where-does-it -come-from-who-does-it-affect.

15. K. Rawlinson, "Windrush: 11 People Wrongly Deported from UK Have Died—Javid," *Guardian*, November 12, 2018, www.theguardian.com/uk -news/2018/nov/12/windrush-11-people-wrongly-deported-from-uk-have -died-sajid-javid.

16. "Home Secretary Apologises to Members of Windrush Generation," Home Office (UK), June 10, 2019, www.gov.uk/government/news/home -secretary-apologises-to-members-of-windrush-generation.

17. M. Ritsner and A. Ponizovsky, "Psychological Distress Through Immigration: The Two-Phase Temporal Pattern?," *International Journal of Social Psychiatry* 45, no. 2 (1999): 125–39.

18. V. Vivero and R. Jenkins, "Existential Hazards of the Multicultural Individual: Defining and Understanding 'Cultural Homelessness,'" *Cultural Diversity and Ethnic Minority Psychology* 5, no. 1 (1999): 6–26.

Chapter 4—Black Bodies

1. G. Kinouani, "Whiteness, Sovereignty and the Body," Race Relations, September 21, 2020, racereflections.co.uk/whiteness-sovereignty-and-the -body.

2. K. Kellaway, "Claudia Rankine: 'Blackness in the White Imagination Has Nothing to Do with Black People,'" *Guardian*, December 27, 2015, www .theguardian.com/books/2015/dec/27/claudia-rankine-poet-citizen -american-lyric-feature.

3. J. Sanburn, "All the Ways Darren Wilson Described Being Afraid of Michael Brown." *Time*, November 25, 2014, time.com/3605346/darren -wilson-michael-brown-demon.

4. Frantz Fanon, *Black Skin, White Masks* (London: Paladin, 1970).

5. Anthony Bateman and Jeremy Holmes, *Introduction to Psychoanalysis: Contemporary Theory and Practice* (London: Routledge, 1995).

6. E. Shohat, "Notes on the 'Post-Colonial,'" *Social Text*, no. 31/32 (1992): 99–113.

7. Joel Feinberg, *The Moral Limits of the Criminal Law*, vol. 3, *Harm to Self* (New York: Oxford University Press, 1989).

8. G. Kinouani, "Brexit, the Body and Politics of the Splitting," Race Reflections, January 26, 2019, racereflections.co.uk/brexit-the-body-politics-of -splitting.

9. B. Stobo, "Location of Disturbance with a Focus on Race, Difference and Culture," master's thesis, Birkbeck College, UK, 2005.
10. Sara Ahmed, *Living a Feminist Life* (Durham, NC: Duke University Press, 2017).
11. R. Eisenman, "Scapegoating and Social Control," *Journal of Psychology* 61, no. 2 (1965): 203–9; Charlie Campbell, *Scapegoat: A History of Blaming Other People* (London: Duckworth Overlook, 2011).
12. Joseph Sandler, "The Concept of Projective Identification," in *Projection, Identification, Projective Identification*, ed. Joseph Sandler (London: Karmac Books, 1988).
13. K. M. Magruder, K. A. McLaughlin, and D. L. Elmore Borbon, "Trauma Is a Public Health Issue," *European Journal of Psychotraumatology* 8, no. 1 (2017): 1375338–39; B. Range, D. Gutierrez, C. Gamboni, N. A. Hough, and A. Wojciak, "Mass Trauma in the African American Community: Using Multiculturalism to Build Resilient Systems," *Contemporary Family Therapy* 40, no. 3 (2018): 284–98.
14. N. Afari, S. M. Ahumada, L. J. Wright, S. Mostoufi, G. Golnari, V. Reis, and J. G. Cuneo, "Psychological Trauma and Functional Somatic Syndromes: A Systematic Review and Meta-Analysis," *Psychosomatic Medicine* 76, no. 1 (2014): 2–11; A. Heenan, P. S. Greenman, V. Tassé, F. Zachariades, and H. Tulloch, "Traumatic Stress, Attachment Style, and Health Outcomes in Cardiac Rehabilitation Patients," *Frontiers in Psychology* 22 (2020): 75.
15. J. Jackson, "Racism and Cardiovascular Disease: Implications for Practice," *Canadian Journal of Cardiology* 31, no. 10 (2015): S314; C. Bell, J. Kerr, and J. Young, "Associations Between Obesity, Obesogenic Environments, and Structural Racism Vary by County-Level Racial Composition," *International Journal of Environmental Research and Public Health* 16, no. 5 (2019): 861; D. Arigo, V. Juth, P. Trief, K. Wallston, J. Ulbrecht, and J. M. Smyth, "Unique Relations Between Post-Traumatic Stress Disorder Symptoms and Patient Functioning in Type 2 Diabetes," *Journal of Health Psychology* 25, no. 5 (2020): 652–64; R. Bayley-Veloso, Y. Z. Szabo, E. Cash, L. Zimmaro, C. Siwik, G. Kloecker, P. Salmon, K. van der Gryp, et al., "The Association Between History of Traumatic Events and Health-Related Quality of Life Among Lung Cancer Patients," *Journal of Psychosocial Oncology* 38, no. 5 (2020): 627–34.
16. American Cancer Society, *Cancer Facts and Figures for African Americans, 2019–2021* (Atlanta: American Cancer Society, 2019).
17. F. Chinegwundoh, "Time to Talk About the Prostate Cancer Risk in Black Men and What We Can Do About It," National Health Service (England), June 12, 2018, https://www.england.nhs.uk/blog/time-to-talk-about-the-prostate-cancer-risk-in-black-men-and-what-we-can-do-about-it.
18. D. H. Chae et al., "Racial Discrimination and Telomere Shortening Among African Americans: The Coronary Artery Risk Development in Young Adults (CARDIA) Study," *Health Psychology* 39, no. 3 (2020): 209–19.

19. A. D. Thames, M. R. Irwin, E. C. Breen, and S. W. Cole, "Experienced Discrimination and Racial Differences in Leukocyte Gene Expression," *Psychoneuroendocrinology* 106 (2020): 277–83; D. B. Lee, E. S. Kim, and E. W. Neblett Jr., "The Link Between Discrimination and Telomere Length in African American Adults," *Health Psychology* 36, no. 5 (2020): 458–67; S. Segerstrom and G. Miller, "Psychological Stress and the Human Immune System: A Meta-Analytic Study of 30 Years Inquiry," *Psychological Bulletin* 130, no. 4 (2006): 601–30.

20. S. Jie Yong, "How Racism Provokes Cellular Ageing, Stress, and Inflammation," *Medium*, June 10, 2020, medium.com/the-faculty/how-racism -provokes-cellular-ageing-stress-and-inflammation-17afece56def.

21. University of Southern California, "Racism Has a Toxic Effect: Study May Explain How Racial Discrimination Raises the Risks of Disease Among African Americans," *ScienceDaily*, May 31, 2019; S. Barber, "Death by Racism," *Lancet Infectious Diseases*, 20, no. 8 (2020): 903; S. R. Liu and S. Modir, "The Outbreak That Was Always Here: Racial Trauma in the Context of COVID-19 and Implications for Mental Health Providers," *Psychological Trauma* 12, no. 5 (2020): 439–42.

22. W. Powell, J. Richmond, D. Mohottige, I. Yen, A. Joslyn, and G. Corbie-Smith, "Medical Mistrust, Racism, and Delays in Preventive Health Screening Among African American Men," *Behavioral Medicine* 45, no. 2 (2019): 102; Y. Hong, J. Tauscher, and M. Cardel, "Distrust in Health Care and Cultural Factors Are Associated with Uptake of Colorectal Cancer Screening in Hispanic and Asian Americans," *Cancer* 124, no. 2 (2018): 335–45.

23. G. Mingucci, "René Descartes' Parricide: The Challenge of Cartesian Philosophy of Nature and Philosophy of Mind to Aristotle's Authorship," *Societateşi Politică*, 12, no. 1 (2018): 81–100; Kinouani, "Brexit, the Body and the Politics of Splitting."

24. Items 1–4, generally, are from P. Beim, "The Disparities in Healthcare for Black Women," Endometriosis Foundation, June 6, 2020, https://www .endofound.org/the-disparities-in-healthcare-for-black-women; item 1: L. G. Blount, "Tackling Black Maternal Mortality in a Pandemic and Beyond," Black Women's Health Imperative, May 26, 2020, https://bwhi.org /2020/05/26/tackling-black-maternal-mortality-in-a-pandemic-and -beyond; item 5: N. Badreldin, W. Grobman, and L. M. Yee, "Racial Disparities in Postpartum Pain Management," *Obstetrics and Gynecology* 134, no. 6 (2019): 1147–53, https://journals.lww.com/greenjournal/Fulltext /2019/12000/Racial_Disparities_in_Postpartum_Pain_Management .4.aspx.

Chapter 5—Raising Black Children

1. G. Kinouani, "On Schools, Institutional Racism and Everyday Violence," Race Reflections, June 22, 2019, https://racereflections.co.uk/articles/page/3.

2. Shirley A. Hill, *African American Children: Socialization and Development in Families* (Thousand Oaks, CA: SAGE Publications, 1999).
3. For items 1–3: K. Quick, "School Discipline Without Racial Equity Is Discrimination," Century Foundation, May 21, 2018, https://tcf.org/content /commentary/school-discipline-without-racial-equity-discrimination.
4. For items 4–9: K. Weir, "Inequality at School: What's Behind the Racial Disparity in Our Education System?," *Monitor on Psychology* 47, no. 10 (2016): 42, https://www.apa.org/monitor/2016/11/cover-inequality -school. Additionally, for item 5: W. S. Gilliam, "Prekindergarteners Left Behind: Expulsion Rates in State Prekindergarten Programs," *FCD Policy Brief* (Foundation for Child Development), May 2005, https://challenging behavior.cbcs.usf.edu/docs/prekindergarteners-left-behind_expulsion-in -state-programs.pdf; for item 6: J. Okonofua and J. Eberhardt, "Two Strikes: Race and the Disciplining of Young Students," *Psychological Science* (April 8, 2015): 617–24; for item 8: S. Nicholson-Crotty, J. A. Grissom, J. Nicholson-Crotty, C. Redding, "Disentangling the Causal Mechanisms of Representative Bureaucracy: Evidence from Assignment of Students to Gifted Programs," *Journal of Public Administration Research and Theory* 26, no. 4 (October 2016): 745–57; for item 9: S. Gershenson, S. B. Holt, and N. W. Papageorge, "Who Believes in Me? The Effect of Student–Teacher Demographic Match on Teacher Expectations," *Economics of Education Review* 52 (June 2016): 209–24.
5. C. H. Burt, R. L. Simons, and F. X. Gibbons, "Racial Discrimination, Ethnic-Racial Socialization, and Crime: A Micro-Sociological Model of Risk and Resilience," *American Sociological Review* 77, no. 4 (2012): 648–77; G. Hurst, "Primary Schools Suspend 40% More Pupils for Racist Behaviour," *Times* (UK), January 2, 2020, www.thetimes.co.uk/article /primary-schools-suspend-40-more-pupils-for-racist-behaviour-rrwh66mpt.
6. K. McGrew, "The Dangers of Pipeline Thinking: How the School-to-Prison Pipeline Metaphor Squeezes Out Complexity," *Educational Theory* 66, no. 3 (2016): 341–67.
7. *The Stephen Lawrence Enquiry: Report of an Inquiry by Sir William Macpherson of Cluny* (Government of the United Kingdom, 1999), assets. publishing.service.gov.uk/government/uploads/system/uploads/attachment _data/file/277111/4262.pdf.
8. J. Levs, "No, Most Black Kids Are Not Fatherless," *HuffPost*, July 27, 2017.
9. Daniel Geary, *Civil Rights: The Moynihan Report and Its Legacy* (Philadelphia: University of Pennsylvania Press, 2015).
10. Harriette Pipes McAdoo, *Black Families*, 3rd ed. (London: SAGE, 1997); Claudia Bernard and Perlita Harris, *Safeguarding Black Children: Good Practice in Child Protection* (London: Jessica Kingsley, 2016).
11. "David Lammy MP Says Absent Fathers 'Key Cause of Knife Crime,'" BBC News, October 3, 2012, www.bbc.co.uk/news/uk-england-london -19815831.

12. R. C. Kessler, K. A. McLaughlin, J. G. Green, M. J. Gruber, N. A. Sampson, A. M. Zaslavsky, S. Aguilar-Gaxiola, et al., "Childhood Adversities and Adult Psychopathology in the WHO World Mental Health Surveys," *British Journal of Psychiatry* 197, no. 5 (2010): 378–85.

13. N. R. Norrick, "Collaborative Remembering in Conversational Narration," *Topics in Cognitive Science* 11, no. 4 (2019): 733–51.

14. M. Ritter, "Silence as the Voice of Trauma," *American Journal of Psychoanalysis* 74, no. 2 (2014): 176.

15. G. Lopez, "Black Parents Describe 'The Talk' They Give to Their Children About the Police," *Vox*, August 8, 2016, www.vox.com/2016/8/8/12401792/police-Black-parents-the-talk.

16. S. Feay, "The School That Tried to End Racism, Channel 4—Can Bias Be Reprogrammed?," *Financial Times*, June 19, 2020.

17. "International Migration," Office for National Statistics, 2011, www.ons.gov.uk/peoplepopulationandcommunity/populationandmigration/internationalmigration.

18. S. Osunami and M. Keneally, "Baltimore Protests: What Smacked Baltimore Teen Has to Say About His Mom," ABC News, April 30, 2015, https://abcnews.go.com/US/baltimore-protests-boy-smacked-mom-cares/story?id=30698915.

19. Angela McCarthy and Catharine Coleborne, *Migration, Ethnicity, and Mental Health: International Perspectives, 1840–2010* (New York: Routledge, 2012).

20. David Ingleby, ed., *Forced Migration and Mental Health: Rethinking the Care of Refugees and Displaced Persons* (New York: Springer, 2005); M. Anderson and G. Lopez, "Key Facts About Black Immigrants in the U.S.," Pew Research Center, January 24, 2018, www.pewresearch.org/fact-tank/2018/01/24/key-facts-about-Black-immigrants-in-the-u-s; R. Feltz, "Black Migrants More Likely to Be Deported," *Guardian*, October 16, 2006, www.theguardian.com/us-news/2016/oct/03/Black-immigrants-us-deportation-rates-criminal-convictions.

21. G. Kinouani, "Death by a Thousand Cuts: A Phenomenological Investigation of People of African Descent in the UK," unpublished paper.

22. Carol Garhart Mooney, *Theories of Attachment: An Introduction to Bowlby, Ainsworth, Gerber, Brazelton, Kennell, and Klaus* (St. Paul, MN: Redleaf Press, 2010).

23. Mary D. Salter Ainsworth, Mary Blehar, Everett Waters, and Sally N. Wall, *Patterns of Attachment: A Psychological Study of the Strange Situation*, classic ed. (New York: Psychology Press/Taylor & Francis, 2015).

24. Fanny Brewster, *Archetypal Grief: Slavery's Legacy of Intergenerational Child Loss* (New York: Routledge, 2019).

25. S. L. Speight, "Internalized Racism: One More Piece of the Puzzle," *Counselling Psychologist* 35, no. 1 (2007): 126–34.

26. W. E. B. Du Bois, *The Souls of Black Folk: Essays and Sketches* (1903) (Amherst: University of Massachusetts Press, 2018).

27. L. M. L. Distel, A. H. Egbert, A. M. Bohnert, and C. D. Santiago, "Chronic Stress and Food Insecurity: Examining Key Environmental Family Factors Related to Body Mass Index Among Low-Income Mexican-Origin Youth," *Family and Community Health* 42, no. 3 (2019): 213–20.

28. Derald Wing Sue, *Race Talk and the Conspiracy of Silence: Understanding and Facilitating Difficult Dialogues on Race* (London: John Wiley & Sons, 2016).

29. K. R. Osborne, M. O. Caughy, A. Oshri, E. P. Smith, and M. T. Owen, "Racism and Preparation for Bias Within African American Families," *Cultural Diversity and Ethnic Minority Psychology* 27, no. 2 (2021): 269–79; J. R. Graham, L. M. West, and L. Roemer, "The Experience of Racism and Anxiety Symptoms in an African-American Sample: Moderating Effects of Trait Mindfulness," *Mindfulness* 4, no. 4 (2013): 332–41.

30. P. A. Goff, M. C. Jackson, B. A. L. Di Leone, B. A. Lewis, C. M. Culotta, and N. A. DiTomasso, "The Essence of Innocence: Consequences of Dehumanizing Black Children," *Journal of Personality and Social Psychology* 106, no. 4 (2014): 526–45.

31. S. Haylock, T. Boshari, E. C. Alexander, A. Kumar, L. Manikam, and R. Pinder, "Risk Factors Associated with Knife-Crime in United Kingdom Among Young People Aged 10–24 Years: A Systematic Review," *BMC Public Health* 20, article 1451 (2020).

Chapter 6—Working While Black

1. P. Newkirk, "Diversity Has Become a Booming Business. So Where Are the Results?," *Time*, October 10, 2019, time.com/5696943/diversity -business.

2. Claire Alexander and Jason Arday, *Aiming Higher: Race, Inequality and Diversity in the Academy* (London: Runnymede Trust, 2015).

3. "Student Record 2017–18," HESA (Higher Education Statistics Agency), 2018, www.hesa.ac.uk/collection/c17051.

4. "Black Workers with Degrees Earn a Quarter Less Than White Counterparts, Finds TUC," Trades Union Congress, February 1, 2016, https:// www.tuc.org.uk/news/black-workers-degrees-earn-quarter-less-white -counterparts-finds-tuc.

5. M. Jameel and J. Yerardi, "Workplace Discrimination Is Illegal. But Our Data Shows It Is Still a Huge Problem," *Vox*, February 29, 2019, www.vox .com/policy-and-politics/2019/2/28/18241973/workplace-discrimination -cpi-investigation-eeoc.

6. R. Awori, "Victory for Lettia McNickle: I Am Not My Hair," *Montreal Community Contact*, December 10, 2018, montrealcommunitycontact .com/lettias-hairstyle-a-problem-at-madisons.

7. Ayana D. Byrd and Lori L. Tharps, *Hair Story: Untangling the Roots of Black Hair in America* (New York: St. Martin's Press, 2002).

8. Emma Dabiri, *Don't Touch My Hair* (London: Penguin, 2019).

9. A. Krivkovich, M. Nadeau, K. Robinson, N. Robinson, I. Starikova, and L. Yee, *Women in the Workplace Report* (McKinsey and Company, 2018), https://www.mckinsey.com/~/media/McKinsey/Featured%20Insights/Gender%20Equality/Women%20in%20the%20Workplace%202019/Women-in-the-workplace-2019.ashx.

10. Kalwant Bhopal, *White Privilege: The Myth of a Post-Racial Society* (Bristol: Policy Press, 2018).

11. S. J. Spencer, C. M. Steele, and D. M. Quinn, "Stereotype Threat and Women's Math Performance," *Journal of Experimental Social Psychology* 35, no. 1 (1999): 4–28.

12. Claude Steele, "Stereotype-Threat and African American Student Achievement," in *The Inequality Reader: Contemporary and Foundational Readings in Race, Class, and Gender*, 2nd ed., ed. David B. Grusky and Szonja Szelenyi (New York: Routledge, 2011).

13. Claude M. Steele and Joshua Aronson, "Stereotype Threat and the Test Performance of Academically Successful African Americans," in *The Black-White Test Score Gap*, ed. Christopher Jencks and Meredith Phillips, 401–27 (Washington, DC: Brookings Institution Press, 1988).

14. J. L. Bratter, K. J. Rowley, and I. Chukhray, "Does a Self-Affirmation Intervention Reduce Stereotype Threat in Black and Hispanic High Schools?," *Race and Social Problems* 8 (2016): 340–56.

15. J. Bullock, T. Lockspeiser, A. Del Pino-Jones, R. Richards, A. Teherani, and K. E. Hauer, "They Don't See a Lot of People My Color: A Mixed Methods Study of Racial/Ethnic Stereotype Threat Among Medical Students on Core Clerkships," *Academic Medicine* 95 (2020): S58–S66, doi: 10.1097/ACM.0000000000003628.

16. D. R. Nadler and M. Komarraju, "Negating Stereotype Threat: Autonomy Support and Academic Identification Boost Performance of African American College Students," *Journal of College Student Development* 57, no. 6 (2016): 667–79, doi:10.1353/csd.2016.0039; P. R. Clance and S. A. Imes, "The Imposter Phenomenon in High Achieving Women: Dynamics and Therapeutic Intervention," *Psychotherapy: Theory, Research and Practice* 15, no. 3 (1978): 241–47, doi.org/10.1037/h0086006; Robbie Shilliam, "Black Academia: The Doors Have Been Opened but the Architecture Remains the Same," in Alexander and Arday, *Aiming Higher*; S. L. Sellers, H. W. Neighbors, and V. L. Bonham, "Goal-Striving Stress and the Mental Health of College-Educated Black American Men: The Protective Effects of System-Blame," *American Journal of Orthopsychiatry* 81, no. 4 (2011): 507–18; S. A. James, N. L. Keenan, D. S. Strogatz, S. R. Browning, and J. M. Garrett, "Socioeconomic Status, John Henryism, and Blood Pressure in Black Adults:

The Pitt County Study," *American Journal of Epidemiology* 135, no. 1 (1992): 59–67.

Chapter 6—Black Love

1. Kenneth B. Clark and Mamie P. Clark, "Racial Identification and Preferences in Negro Children," in *Readings in Social Psychology*, ed. Theodore M. Newcomb and Eugene L. Hartley (New York: Holt, 1947).
2. L. Dickey-Bryant, G. J. Lautenschlager, J. L. Mendoza, and N. Abrahams, "Facial Attractiveness and Its Relation to Occupational Success," *Journal of Applied Psychology* 71, no. 1 (1986): 16–19.
3. E. Chito Childs, "Looking Behind the Stereotypes of the 'Angry Black Woman,'" *Gender and Society* 19, no. 4 (2005): 544–61.
4. L. Bland, "Interracial Relationships and the 'Brown Baby Question': Black GIs, White British Women, and Their Mixed-Race Offspring in World War II," *Journal of the History of Sexuality* 26, no. 3 (2017): 424–53.
5. Office for National Statistics (UK), "2011 Census Analysis: What Does the 2011 Census Tell Us About Inter-Ethnic Relationships?," www.ons .gov.uk.
6. G. Livingston and A. Brown, "Trends and Patterns in Intermarriage," Pew Research Center, May 18, 2017, www.pewsocialtrends.org/2017/05/18 /1-trends-and-patterns-in-intermarriage.
7. B. C. Cruz and M. J. Berson, "The American Melting Pot? Miscegenation Laws in the United States," *OAH Magazine of History* 15, no. 4: (2001): 80–84. www.jstor.org/stable/25163474.
8. D. A. Hollinger, "The One Drop Rule and the One Hate Rule," *Daedalus* 134, no. 1 (2005): 18–28.
9. N. Nayabola, "Satoshi Kanazawa's Racist Nonsense Should Not Be Tolerated," *Guardian*, May 18, 2011, www.theguardian.com/commentisfree /2011/may/18/satoshi-kanazawa-Black-women-psychology-today.
10. Lauren Michele Jackson, *White Negroes: When Cornrows Were in Vogue . . . and Other Thoughts on Cultural Appropriation* (Boston: Beacon Press, 2019).
11. Patricia Hill Collins, *Black Feminist Thought: Knowledge, Consciousness, and the Politics of Empowerment*, 2nd ed. (New York: Routledge, 2000).
12. E. Dabiri, "Who Stole All the Black Women from Britain?," Media Diversified, November 5, 2013, mediadiversified.org/2013/11/05/who-stole -all-the-Black-women-from-britain; S. A. James, N. L. Keenan, D. S. Strogatz, S. R. Browning, and J. M. Garrett, "Socioeconomic Status, John Henryism, and Blood Pressure in Black Adults: The Pitt County Study," *American Journal of Epidemiology* 135, no. 1 (1992): 59–67.
13. Daniel P. Moynihan, *The Negro Family: The Case for National Action* (Washington, DC: Office of Policy Planning and Research, US Department of Labor, 1965); J. Washington, "Blacks Struggle with 72 Percent Unwed Mothers Rate," NBC News, November 7, 2010, www.nbcnews .com/id/wbna39993685#.URXHo80hclk.

14. T. Brown and E. Patterson, "Wounds from Incarceration That Never Heal," *New Republic*, June 28, 2016, newrepublic.com/article/134712 /wounds-incarceration-never-heal.

15. H. A. Williams, "How Slavery Affected African American Families," National Humanities Center, http://nationalhumanitiescenter.org/tserve /freedom/1609-1865/essays/aafamilies.htm, accessed May 23, 2021.

16. Frantz Fanon, *Black Skin, White Masks* (London: Paladin, 1970).

17. N. Appelbaum, "Whitening the Region: Caucano Mediation and 'Antioqueño Colonization' in Nineteenth-Century Colombia," *Hispanic American Historical Review* 79, no. 4 (1999): 631–67, doi: 10.1215/00182168 -79.4.631.

18. B. Jones and M. J. Hill, "African American Lesbians, Gay Men, and Bisexuals," in *Textbook of Homosexuality and Mental Health*, ed. Robert P. Cabaj and Terry S. Stein, 549–61 (Washington, DC: American Psychiatric Association, 1996).

19. B. M'Baye, "The Origins of Senegalese Homophobia: Discourses on Homosexuals and Transgender People in Colonial and Postcolonial Senegal," *African Studies Review* 56, no. 2 (2013): 109–28.

20. T. A. Foster, "The Sexual Abuse of Black Men Under American Slavery," *Journal of the History of Sexuality* 20, no. 3 (2011): 445–64.

21. R. G. Dudley, "Being Black and Lesbian, Gay, Bisexual or Transgender," *Journal of Gay and Lesbian Mental Health* 17, no. 2 (2013): 183–95.

Chapter 8—Black Resistance

1. Southern Poverty Law Center, "Civil Rights Martyrs," www.splcenter.org /what-we-do/civil-rights-memorial/civil-rights-martyrs, accessed May 23, 2021.

2. Suman Fernando, *Institutional Racism in Psychiatry and Clinical Psychology: Race Matters in Mental Health* (Cham, Switzerland: Palgrave Macmillan, 2017); K. McKenzie and K. Bhui, "Institutional Racism in Mental Health Care," *British Medical Journal* 334 (2007): 649–50; L. Polanco-Roman, A. Danies, and D. M. Anglin, "Racial Discrimination as Race-Based Trauma, Coping Strategies, and Dissociative Symptoms Among Emerging Adults," *Psychological Trauma: Theory, Research, Practice and Policy* 8, no. 5 (2016): 609–17, doi:10.1037/tra0000125.

3. Claire Raymond, *Witnessing Sadism in Texts of the American South: Women, Specularity, and the Poetics of Subjectivity* (Surrey, UK: Ashgate Publishing, 2014).

4. Reni Eddo-Lodge, *Why I'm No Longer Talking to White People About Race* (London: Bloomsbury Publishing, 2017).

5. "Black Studies Center Public Dialogue. Pt. 2," panel session featuring Toni Morrison, Portland State Library Special Collections, May 30, 1975, available at soundcloud.com/portland-state-library/portland-state-Black -studies-1?mc_cid=7a27cfd978&mc_eid=e2efbcffa9.

6. Deborah Gabriel, *Layers of Blackness: Colourism in the African Diaspora* (London: Imani Media, 2007).

7. Eddo-Lodge, *Why I'm No Longer Talking to White People About Race*, ix.

8. Association for Dance Movement Psychotherapy UK, admp.org.uk.

9. C. Sarvan, "The Term 'Racism' and Discourse," *Journal of Commonwealth Literature* 35, no. 2 (2000): 129–39.

10. R. T. Middleton, "Institutions, Inculcation, and Black Racial Identity: Pigmentocracy vs. the Rule of Hypodescent," *Social Identities* 14, no. 5 (2008): 567–85.

11. In Maya Angelou, *And Still I Rise* (London: Virago Press, 1986).

12. E. F. Glick, "Harlem's Queer Dandy: African-American Modernism and the Artifice of Blackness," *Modern Fiction Studies* 49, no. 3 (2003): 414–42; M. L. Stone, "Congolese Dandies: Meet the Stylish Men and Women of Brazzaville—in Pictures," *Guardian*, August 27, 2020.

13. bell hooks, *Black Looks: Race and Representation* (Boston: South End Press, 1992).

14. G. Kinouani, "Beauty as Resistance: On Marginalisation, Style & Self-Love," Race Reflections, January 17, 2016, racereflections.co.uk/beaut y-as-resistance-on-marginalisation-style-self-love.

15. S. C. Scott, "Black Excellence: Fostering Intellectual Curiosity in Minority Honors Students at a Predominantly White Research Institution," *Journal of the National Collegiate Honors Council* 18, no. 1 (2017): 109–33.

16. B. D. Lozenski, "Beyond Mediocrity: The Dialectics of Crisis in the Continuing Miseducation of Black Youth," *Harvard Educational Review* 87, no. 2 (2017): 161–85.

17. G. Kinouani, "Shame and Marginalisation: An Intersubjective Formulation Model," Race Reflections, October 18, 2015, racereflections.co.uk /shame-and-marginalisation-an-intersubjective-formulation-model; Frantz Fanon, *Black Skin, White Masks* (London: Paladin, 1970).

18. A. J. Johnson and J. Wakefield, "Examining Associations Between Racism, Internalized Shame, and Self-Esteem Among African Americans," *Cogent Psychology* 7, no. 1 (2020).

19. J. W. Berry, "Acculturation: A Conceptual Overview," in *Acculturation and Parent–Child Relationships: Measurement and Development*, ed. Marc H. Bornstein and Linda R. Cote, 13–30 (Mahwah, NJ: Lawrence Erlbaum Associates, 2006).

20. Quoted in John Frederick Walker, *A Certain Curve of Horn: The Hundred-Year Quest for the Giant Sable Antelope of Angola* (London: Grove Press, 2004), 144. It must be noted that the origin of the quote remains contested.

21. Luis Lugo and Alan Cooperman, *Tolerance and Tension: Islam and Christianity in Sub-Saharan Africa* (Pew Research Center, 2010), https://www .pewforum.org/2010/04/15/executive-summary-islam-and-christianity -in-sub-saharan-africa.

22. C. Ebersohl, "Religion and Resistance in Enslaved Communities," Virginia Center for Civil War Studies, 2017, civilwar.vt.edu/religion-and -resistance-in-enslaved-communities; K. C. Nweke and I. P. Okpaleke, "The Re-emergence of African Spiritualities: Prospects and Challenges," *Transformation: An International Journal of Holistic Mission Studies* 36, no. 4 (2019): 246–65.

23. Christopher C. H. Cook, *Recommendations for Psychiatrists on Spirituality and Religion: Position Statement* (Royal College of Psychiatrists, November 2013), www.rcpsych.ac.uk/pdf/ps03_2013.pdf.

24. G. Kinouani, "Finding Black Joy Amidst Black Pain," Race Reflections, August 11, 2019, https://racereflections.co.uk/2019/08/; Raymond, *Witnessing Sadism in Texts of the American South.*

25. W. E. B. Du Bois, *The Souls of Black Folk: Essays and Sketches* (1903) (Amherst: University of Massachusetts Press, 2018).

26. P. Freire, "Cultural Action and Conscientization," *Harvard Educational Review* 4, no. 3 (1970): 452–77.

27. M. E. P. Seligman, "Learned Helplessness," *Annual Review of Medicine* 23 (1972): 407–12.

28. K. Neff, "Definition of Self-Compassion," Self-Compassion, 2021, self-compassion.org/the-three-elements-of-self-compassion-2; K. Neff, "Self-Compassion: An Alternative Conceptualization of a Healthy Attitude Toward Oneself," *Self and Identity* 2, no. 2 (2003): 85–101, doi.org/10 .1080/15298860309032.

29. D. Wilson, "Competency, Connectedness, and Consciousness," in *"We Ain't Crazy! Just Coping with a Crazy System": Pathways into the Black Population for Eliminating Mental Health Disparities,* ed. V. Diane Woods, Nicelma J. King, Suzanne Midori Hanna, and Carolyn Murray (San Bernardino, CA: African American Health Institute of San Bernardino County, 2012), 159–61.

INDEX